NEW OPPORTUNITIES IN A NEW NATION

The Development of New York
After the Revolution

Edited by

Manfred Jonas and Robert V. Wells

DEPARTMENT OF HISTORY
UNION COLLEGE

in cooperation with
UNION COLLEGE PRESS
Schenectady, NY 1982

New Opportunities in a New Nation: The Development of New York
after the Revolution

Copyright © 1982 Union College

Published by Union College Schenectady, New York 12308, U.S.A.

Distributed by Syracuse University Press, Syracuse, New York, 13210, U.S.A.

Library of Congress Catalog Number: 82-50939

To

Samuel B. Fortenbaugh, Jr.

Trustee of Union College and Historian of its Founding

CONTENTS

PREFACE:

ANATOMY OF A CONFERENCE

MANFRED JONAS

The offer of Patroni Scholastici, a private foundation devoted to the encouragement of scholarship, to provide funds for a conference to be organized by Union College's Department of History set in motion a train of events of which the publication of this volume is the culminating, but hopefully not final one. The foundation neither stipulated nor suggested a subject but set its only condition that the money it made available be matched by Union College.

The offer presented the History Department with both a challenge and an opportunity. What could be done on a modest scale which held the promise of success as an event, and would make a genuine contribution to the advancement of scholarship, both in itself and through the stimulation it would provide? After considerable deliberation it was concluded that a conference on a subject of regional interest and some logical relationship to the sponsoring institution would be most likely to draw both participants and an audience. In order to secure substantial original contributions and to disseminate the results as widely as possible, the papers prepared for the conference should ultimately be published.

In line with such considerations, it was decided to hold a conference focussing on the development of New York after the American Revolution, i.e. during the period in which Union College was founded, to identify and invite four individuals who were engaged in significant research in this field, and to provide for discussion and interaction among all of the participants on the basis of original papers to be presented by the invited scholars. Since the subject selected was hardly narrow and the various papers might thus have sharply differing foci, it seemed desirable to ask one of these scholars to prepare, as his or her contribution, a paper based on the other three and bringing them, if at all possible, towards a common theme. We were remarkably fortunate that Michael Kammen, not only the author of a history of colonial New York but a Pulitzer Prize winning historian, agreed to undertake this task before either the other participants or their possible subjects had been determined. For his initial daring and subsequent accomplishment we are, of course, most grateful.

Having thus established the parameters within which the conference would function and, not incidentally, secured a "drawing card" which could be expected to attract additional participants, we attempted to identify other individuals who were engaged in significant scholarly work dealing with the subject of the conference. In this effort we had the gracious assistance of the New York State Education Department, particularly of its Supervisor of History Research, Stefan Bielinski, and of a network of scholars which grew as specific individuals were contacted.

Our original intention was to seek papers on such different but not unrelated subjects as constitutional development, the progress of education, the changing roles of women, and the growth of industry and commerce. This intention was modified as the areas in which important work was being done became more clearly defined, and as the availability of individual scholars—or their non-availability—became apparent. Since we insisted on new and unpublished research and had, given the need for our "integrator" to read and digest the other papers before beginning his, some rather rigid and short-term deadlines for submission of papers, our pool shrank rapidly—in quantity but not in quality.

Very early in the proceedings we had decided to bring to the conference, if at all possible, the perspective of someone who was not a historian, but who would treat issues of interest to historians from a complementary point of view. Our first choice, in that respect, was for a cultural geographer. Here too we proved fortunate, for Donald Meinig, who after producing superb regional studies of the American West had turned his attention increasingly to New York State and had recently sought to build a bridge between historians and geographers in an article in the *American Historical Review*, was the second scholar to accept our invitation.

When Mary-Jo Kline, an accomplished historical editor whose talents and interest in New York had been honed on both the papers of Aaron Burr and the career of Gouverneur Morris, then offered to contribute a paper on the political realities encountered in pulling a geographically, economically and culturally divided area together into a state, the contours of our conference had been established. What remained was to find someone whose focus would not be on New York in its regional setting, nor yet on creating unity of the diversity within the new state, but who would bring to our deliberations the results of the study of a particular segment of that entity we call New York. When the exhaustive work on the Genesee country and its settlement which had engaged the attention of William Siles for many years came to our attention, we knew we had found the missing piece for a conference which, while true to our original intention to strive for a diversity of perspectives, would have a degree of thematic unity for which we had scarcely dared to hope.

Once the key participants had been committed, it remained to work out a format that would allow for the highest degree of interaction among them, as well as between them and the others who would attend the conference. Since interest in the subject was our sole attraction, it was clear that the meeting had to be relatively short. Moreover, the sessions would have to be held at convenient hours so as to minimize interference with other activities and to hold down expenses for the participants. In order to meet all of these requirements, we scheduled two of the papers for one session beginning in the late afternoon of a Friday, and the third paper for later that evening. Between the two sessions, all

those in attendance were invited to a dinner at which not only discussion about the subject of the conference could be
continued, but genuine contact among all the participants be
established. In a final session on the following morning, the
integrating paper was presented, and discussed by a panel
composed of the previous speakers and the conference
organizers. The general discussion which followed concluded
the conference.

In many respects, the results exceeded our most optimistic
expectations. As the three basic papers came in, one by one,
but surprisingly close to the agreed upon deadlines, we happily recognized that they represented substantial scholarly
contributions. Our "integrator's" initial reaction to them
confirmed that fact. But we had no way of knowing who
would, in fact, attend the conference, and anxiously awaited
the response to our mailing, which had gone to potentially
interested persons within a 250 mile radius of Schenectady.

To identify those person, we had scanned both the mailing
lists made available by the New York State Education
Department and the American Historical Association's
Directory of Departments of History. We hoped for a small
but select group that would more or less fill the site for the
conference, and elegantly furnished lounge which, though
reflecting New York in the nineteeth century rather than in
the eighteenth, provided both a stimulating and comfortable
setting. Though we had asked persons to indicate their intention to attend, only a small trickle of responses was received,
and it was not until the day of event that we were to discover
to what extent our hopes would be realized.

As it turned out, attendance at the various functions rang-
ed from 25 at the dinner (graciously served by the Union College Food Service in the Banquet Room of the Dutch Hollow
Pub) to 40 at the Saturday morning meeting, which even attracted some alumni who took time out from Homecoming
festivities to seek intellectual stimulation. Only four or five of
the persons at each session were from the Union faculty or administration, and the vast majority had come in response to
our invitation from New York, New Jersey, Pennsylvania,
and Massachusetts. Representing the academic profession as

well as historical societies, state agencies or simply personal interest, they proved to be an extraordinarily interesting and interested group, ideally suited for the purpose we had in mind. In the formal sessions and the various informal get-togethers they contributed immeasurably to the success of the enterprise.

So did, in addition to Patroni Scholastici, without whose generosity there would have been no conference, and to others already referred to, President John S. Morris of Union College, who made facilities and funds available for the conference, Jack L. Maranville, without whom there would have been no publication, chairman Donald R. Thurston of the Department of History, and my departmental colleagues Catherine Clinton, who ably handled local arrangements, and Marc H. Dawson, who assisted her.

That the conference was indeed a success is attested to by a number of factors. Not only did all of those involved with the enterprise, in whatever capacity, leave the scene with a sense of satisfaction, a great many left better informed, with newly developed contacts and with new stimulation to carry on their own work. Indeed the idea and the format were regarded as so successful that they were adopted virtually *in toto* by the College's Division of Social Sciences, which is sponsoring a conference on "Japanese Productivity: Lessons for America," at the college this spring. The experience clearly demonstrated the value of a small conference at which, in contrast to the often huge professional meetings, all those attending share a common scholarly interest, and where they are free to interact under conditions designed for stimulation, comfort and convenience. If the present volume serves to involve a wider audience of vicarious participants, the conference's function will have been even better served.

Schenectady, New York   MANFRED JONAS
April 1982

WHAT THEN IS NEW YORK,

THIS NEW STATE?

AN INTRODUCTION

ROBERT V. WELLS

For a variety of reasons, American historians have not always given equal attention to all the times, places, and events that encompass the full sweep of American history. Reflecting matters of taste, inherent interest, and the amount and accessibility of documents, American history is full of "neglected" periods and places, and has some subjects about which there seems little more of significance to be written. In the context of the scholarship about America prior to 1830, New York in the early national period would seem to fit more into the former than the latter category. For the colonial period, the literature on New York is modest in quantity, though not in quality, when compared to the studies of Massachusetts or Virginia. Writing on New York in the period between 1775 and 1830 is also relatively scarce.[1] In view of this, it is appropriate that Union College, founded in upstate New York in 1795, sponsored a symposium in October, 1981, to examine some of the main historical trends in New York in the early years of the new nation. As the results show, the relative neglect of this part of American history cannot be blamed either on a lack of interesting subjects or a

---

1. Some notable exceptions include, David M. Ellis, *Landlords and Farmers in the Hudson-Mohawk Region, 1790-1850* (Ithaca, 1946); *idem.*, "The Yankee Invasion of New York, 1783-1850," *New York History,* 32 (1951), 3-17; Mary P. Ryan, *Cradle of the Middle Class: The Family in Oneida County, New York, 1790-1865* (Cambridge, Eng., 1981); Alfred F. Young, *The Democratic Republicans of New York: The Origins, 1763-1797* (Chapel Hill, 1967).

lack of sources. Here is a time and place that offers ample opportunity for fresh, insightful scholarship.

The question of why New York has not attracted the attention that Massachusetts, Virginia, or even its neighboring middle colony, Pennsylvania, have is one that has at least two broad answers. The first is that, unlike some other colonies or states, New York's history has never been easily presented in the form of a vivid, coherent metaphor that both captures the imagination and simplifies the complexities of the full historical story. Regardless of whether the labels of Puritan, Quaker, or Cavalier or Planter are accurate in depicting the essence of life in Massachusetts, Pennsylvania, or Virginia respectively, these names offer both serious and incidental students convenient hooks upon which to hang the details of history.

New York defies such simplification. From its earliest years, New York was a complex entity composed of contending and contrasting people and regions.[2] By the middle of the seventeenth century, Long Island, New York City, the Hudson Valley, and the area around Albany all had their own distinct traits. In addition, the history of New York is frequently one of trade and commerce, matters that are basic to American history, but which do not enliven the imagination in the same way as do the Puritan experiment and its ultimate failure in Massachusetts, or the tragedies of early Jamestown and the growth of slavery in Virginia. In the case of the Chesapeake colony too, the elegant planters who came to dominate Virginia in the eighteenth century and who provided much of the leadership for the early republic are more appealing than their frequently quarrelsome counterparts who made up the New York elite.

It is a common device to label New York as one of the "middle " colonies or states, along with New Jersey, Pennsylvania, Delaware, and occasionally Maryland. Frequently,

---

2. Thomas J. Archdeacon, *New York City, 1664-1710: Conquest and Change* (Ithaca, 1976); Patricia Bonomi, *A Factious People: Politics and Society in Colonial New York* (New York, 1971); Michael Kammen, *Colonial New York: A History* (New York, 1975).

this reflects nothing more than a lumping of what is perceived to be an ill-defined region between New England and the Chesapeake or the South. Even if the label is used to portray a region of toleration and moderation, which had neither great success nor tragic failure, the story is not one that automatically intrigues us. Much of the appeal of history is in the colorful and the different. Since New York has often been described as the earliest manifestation of what America later became (e.g. pluralistic, individualistic, urban) it lacks the appeal of other more exotic regions.[3]

A second answer to why New York in the early national period has not always received its share of attention from historians revolves around matters that can be linked loosely as part of the sociology of knowledge. Anyone who has ever had to read seventeenth and eighteenth century documents, frequently written by semi-literate individuals not trained in penmanship, understands the effort of research in this period. The frequent use of Dutch in the early New York records has surely encouraged many potential students to turn elsewhere. No university or other institution in the state has done for New York what Harvard and Yale have done for the study of New England, or Colonial Williamsburg for Virginia and the Chesapeake. The presence of New York City within the state provides a lure for potential scholars that is understandable, but perhaps regrettable when it comes to understanding the state as a whole. Just as it is valid to point out that what has been termed American history is often New England (or even eastern Massachusetts) history, so too has the City of New York come to dominate the history of the state. One of the great virtues of this collection of papers is that they avoid this flaw. Finally, New York, as a state, had the misfortune to undergo its period of most rapid growth and development just as the new nation was emerging from

---

3. David M. Ellis, "New York and Middle Atlantic Regionalism," *New York History*, 35 (1954), 3-13; Milton M. Klein, "New York in the American Colonies: A New Look," *New York History*, 53 (1972), 132-156; *idem.*, "Shaping the American Tradition: The Microcosm of Colonial New York," *New York History*, 59 (1978), 173-197.

the wreckage of the first British empire. Not surprisingly, the Revolution, the perils of the Confederation period, the Constitution, and the political struggles of the central government from 1789 to 1815 have frequently proved more attractive than the extraordinary changes in New York during this period.

The papers in this volume offer some fascinating insights into the history of New York during what must be one of the most dynamic and creative periods in the state's past, through perspectives that are different in terms of both subject and scale. Of the first three essays, only Kline's is perhaps truly a history of the state. Siles is concerned with the Genesee Country, while Meinig examines New York both as a collection of regions and as part of a larger whole.

Although Kline's essay, is, at heart, political, it is every bit as exciting and important as the discoveries in social and intellectual history that have made the study of early America so lively over the last two decades. Kline reminds us that the state of New York after 1790 was a distinctly different entity than the colony in 1775. In doing this, she is not so much concerned with constitutional questions, as with the problems political leaders faced after 1790 in trying to govern (and it did have to be governed) a state that was much more extensive in terms of actual settled territory than the colony of the same name, and that included geographic regions which were not naturally linked to the older settlements. This story is important, not only in terms of the state's history, but also in comparison to the experience of other states.

In New England, most of the states were completely settled by the Revolution. Massachusetts, of course, had a northern frontier in what later became Maine, but geography did not produce the centrifugal force in that case that it did in New York. Interestingly, in Virginia and North Carolina, where geography combined with westward migration to encourage separation, Kentucky and Tennessee were quickly established and became a part of the Union. In so doing, they anticipated much of later history when new states emerged from older, and larger territories. This story was repeated from the Northwest Territory to the eventual decision in favor of a "small" California. If we ignore the fact that Vermont emerged from land claimed by New Yorkers, and other states as well, then the story Kline tells is more like the process by which many seventeenth century colonies created viable political units out of disparate parts than anything experienced by the other states in the early national period.

In his study of the settlement of the Genesee country, Siles offers us some detailed insights into many of the processes that interest the other contributors to this volume on a more general level. In addition, he demonstrates how old and new traditions in the study of American history can be combined in productive scholarship. Certainly, the role land speculators played in opening various wests from Massachusetts to the Rockies is a familiar theme to students of American history.[4] Siles, however, is not so much interested in how this fits with the image of a democratic society, as he is in showing how large tracts of public land were transferred into the hands of thousands of individuals. Understanding how American state and national governments sought to do this quickly and with minimum bother to themselves by use of speculators is important not only because it is part of the story of westward migration, but also because of the light it reflects on the political and financial problems of the new governments. The movement of Europeans into western New York is also an important outcome of the War of Independence, since it reversed British policy after 1763, which had tried to limit migration by the colonists into the interior.

When Siles examines the importance of Canandaigua in the plans of the speculators, he makes use of local history to give meaning to his general propositions and shows that in-

---

4. Charles S. Grant, *Democracy in the Connecticut Frontier Town of Kent* (New York, 1961); Robert D. Mitchell, *Commercialism and Frontier: Perspectives on the Early Shenandoah Valley* (Charlottesville, 1977); Allan D. Bogue, *From Prairie to Cornbelt: Farming on the Illinois and Iowa Prairies in the Nineteenth Century* (Chicago, 1963).

fant "cities" were as much a part of the efforts to settle the
western parts of New York as they were in early Massachusetts
or Virginia, in eastern Pennsylvania and the Shenandoah
Valley in the eighteenth century, or in the Ohio Valley and
on the Great Plains during the nineteenth century migrations
into those regions.[5] In New York, as elsewhere, the romantic
image of American expansion by thousands of Daniel
Boones, bear-slayers, must give way to a more accurate ap-
preciation of Boone's more representative role as the founder
of Boonesborough.

There are two obvious ways to expand our understanding
of New York's history. The first is to ask historians what they
have discovered that is new and important; the second is to
ask scholars from other disciplines to examine new or old
historical questions from a different perspective. Since
studies of other colonies and states have already shown the
value of the geographer's perspective to history,[6] and since
Donald Meinig's earlier work was frequently shaped by an interest in the past, he seemed like a natural participant in this
venture.[7] Fortunately, he thought so too.

Although there was no deliberate effort to have it do so,
Meinig's essay complements the studies of Kline and Siles in

---

5. William Haller, Jr., *The Puritan Frontier: Town Planting in New England Col-
onial Development, 1630-1660* (New York, 1951); John C. Rainbolt, "The
Absence of Towns in Seventeenth-Century Virginia," *Journal of Southern
History,* 35 (1969), 343-360; James T. Lemon, *The Best Poor Man's Country: A
Geographical Study of Early Southeastern Pennsylvania* (Baltimore, 1972); Mit-
chell, *Commercialism and Frontier;* Richard C. Wade, *The Urban Frontier:
Pioneer Life in Early Pittsburgh, Cincinnati, Lexington, Louisville, and St. Louis*
(Chicago, 1964); Robert R. Dykstra, *The Cattle Towns* (New York, 1968).
6. Lemon, *op. cit.;* Mitchell, *op. cit.;* Peter O. Wacker, *Land and People: A
Cultural Geography of Pre-industrial New Jersey: Origins and Settlement Patterns* (New Brunswick, 1975).
7. For examples of Mening's historically oriented work, see, "The Mormon
Culture Region: Strategies and Patterns in the Geography of the American West,
1847-1964," *Annals of the Association of American Geographers,* 55 (1965),
191-220; *Imperial Texas: An Interpretive Essay in Cultural Geography* (Austin,
1969); or *Southwest: Three Peoples in Geographical Change, 1600-1970*(New
York, 1971). He is also the author of three of the four historical chapters in John
H. Thompson, ed., *Geography of New York State* (Syracuse, 1966).

some important ways. To begin with, he demonstrates that there are a variety of ways by which New York can be examined as a coherent unit in terms of cultural geography, and offers historians examples of techniques by which they can explore whether a political or geographically well-defined space makes any sense in terms of the people who live there. Interestingly, his study suggests that New York is often best understood either as a collection of regions whose borders do not always exactly match the state's, or as part of some larger section. The fact that he finds ''New York'' hard to define is particularly interesting in view of Kline's reminder that, whatever its composition, New York was a political unit and had to be governed one way or another. Although Meinig is very aware of the influence of perspective, his essay and Siles' combine to remind us that what we see depends on where we stand. In Siles' study, we stand so close that New York disappears, but many trends of American history in general emerge. As Meinig helps us step back from the local details, New York at first becomes clearer, if a bit blurred around the edges, but begins to merge into a larger whole as we continue to back away.

The concluding essay in the volume, by Kammen, is different in two ways. First, he was asked to react to the contributions of Kline, Meinig, and Siles in any way he deemed appropriate, and so had somewhat less freedom regarding his topic than the other authors. Kammen's choice in the manner of his response provides the second difference, for he suggests that in spite of the doubts raised by the other authors, New York may have existed in the early national period as a state of mind as much as anything else. Making use of a variety of sources unlike any exploited by the other authors, Kammen shows us a colony and state inhabited by people who were active, energetic, and optimistic. It does not matter whether the New Yorkers' outlook on life was the result of selective migration, stimulation arising from cultural interaction, the absence of inhibiting forces from the kinds of factors that gave definition to society in Massachusetts and Virginia, or some other cause. What is important is that in-

stead of allowing the problems of a complex society, beset by
some rather impressive external and internal forces, to over-
whelm and depress them, New Yorkers busily took care of
what Kammen refers to as "de-colonization", and then set
forth on the road to becoming the "empire" state. Perhaps
his emphasis can be traced to a greater concern with New
York City than was shown by the other authors, but the
previous papers also suggest a vitality in the state as a whole
that is truly impressive. In fact, the story is remarkable
enough, as these essays show, that it probably would have
received attention comparable to that given to the Puritan
experience or the Virginia planters if it had not occurred just
as the new nation took shape.

All four of these essays emphasize the dramatic expansion
of New York between 1770 and 1830, while raising, in one
form or another the question of whether New York exists as
anything but a political unit. Both the emphasis and the
question are worth further consideration.

Because New York took more censuses during the colonial
period than any of the other colonies that eventually became
part of the United States, it is possible to place the rapid expansion during the early republic in a much broader
demographic context.[8] In 1703, the population of the colony
was just under 21,000; about half a century later, in 1749,
just over 73,000 people lived in New York. The rate of
growth during this period averaged 2.7 per cent each year, a
figure high enough to raise questions about the oft-repeated
statement that large land grants in the colony discouraged
growth. Population increase during the second half of the

---

8. The data on population are derived from Bureau of Census, *U.S. Statistical
Abstract, 1980* (Washington, 1980); *idem., Historical Statistics of the United
States, Bicentennial Edition* (Washington, 1976); Franklin B. Hough, *Census of
the State of New York for 1855* (Albany, 1857); James Potter, "The Growth of
Population in America, 1700-1870," in D. V. Glass and D.E.C. Eversley, eds.,
Population in History (Chicago, 1965); and Robert V. Wells, *Population of the
British Colonies in America before 1776: A Survey of Census Data* (Princeton,
1975). See also, Ruth Higgins, *Expansion in New York with Especial Reference to
the Eighteenth Century* (Columbus, Ohio, 1931) and Chapters 2, 4, and 5 of
Ellis, *Landlords and Farmers.*

century was even more impressive, as an average yearly increase of 4.0 per cent produced a jump in total population from 73,348 to 586,756 between 1749 and 1800. By 1850, the state counted 3,097,394 people, the result of a 3.3 per cent average annual rate of growth in the first half of the nineteenth century. Although the growth rate dropped off between 1850 and 1900 to only (!) 1.7 per cent, the number of men, women, and children living in the state according to the federal census at the turn of the century was 7,268,894, almost 352 times larger than in 1703.

However impressive these figures are in general, the rates of increase for New York during the first years of the new nation are the most noteworthy. Between 1771 and 1830, the overall rate of increase averaged 4.1 per cent each year, with the peak period of growth occurring between 1790 and 1810, when the growth rate was 5.2 per cent annually. Of these years, the decade from 1790 to 1800 saw a yearly increase of 5.5 per cent; the corresponding figure for 1800 to 1810 is 4.9 per cent. Although the rest of the country also grew rapidly during this period, New York's population explosion was such that about 15 per cent of all Americans lived in the state by 1830. During the colonial period, no more than 9 per cent of the people of the future United States had lived in New York, a figure not far below the 9.6 per cent of all Americans living in New York in 1900. Thus, in terms of numbers alone, as well as in the various ways described by the contributors to this volume, New York was a tremendously dynamic part of the new nation.

Because of the presence of New York City, the state is often thought of in predominantly urban terms. This is not entirely inaccurate, especially in the context of American development as a whole, for half the population of the state lived in cities by 1870, fully half a century before the country could make the same claim. Since about one of every four or five inhabitants lived in or around New York City even in the first decades of the eighteenth century, the identification of New York state with urban life apparently began relatively early. Yet when we look closely at the figures for the period

we are most concerned with here, it is surprising to find that
more New Yorkers lived in rural environments during the
years of rapid expansion than at any other time between 1700
and 1900. The first four federal censuses (1790-1820) record-
ed an urban total ranging only from a low of 11.5 per cent in
1790 to a high of 12.8 per cent in 1800. The process that produced record proportions of rural New Yorkers in the early
years of the new nation began about the middle of the eighteenth century as population began to move up the Hudson,
before exploding westward along the Mohawk toward the
Genesee in the years after independence. To be sure, the
state's inhabitants were almost twice as likely to live in cities
as Americans in general. Only 5.0 and 6.1 per cent of the nation's people lived in urban settings in 1790 and 1800,
respectively. And by 1830, the tendency for New Yorkers to
cluster together had reasserted itself as 15.0 per cent of all the
state's residents lived in cities, while in 1840, the urban
population was much the same as at the start of the eighteenth century, about one in five. Nevertheless, as Siles
describes below, new towns like Canandaigua played a role in
the settlement of western New York that made the state
more, rather than less, rural in the years after independence,
as was intended by the community's founders.

In reflecting on the overall significance of the papers by
Kammen, Kline, Meinig, and Siles, and on many of the
details of population patterns in New York state, a useful
analogy to the problem of trying to define New York comes
to mind. Imagine standing close to a large painting on the
wall of a museum. At this distance, what catches the eye may
be the smaller details of the picture, but one also notices such
things as brush strokes, tiny differences in color, and perhaps
places where the edges between one part of the painting and
another are not very distinct. A few steps back brings the
work as a whole into focus. Large areas of color and movement, and the subject of the picture become apparent. The
details take on meaning and come to life. If the museum
staff has been thoughtful, then another few steps back may
reveal the picture to be part of a collection by the same artist,

on the same subject, or from the same period. As a result, the picture takes on additional meaning by being placed in context, even though it loses some of its uniqueness in the process. If the gallery is large and one happens to glance back from a distance, the picture has once again disappeared. It is visible as a spot on the wall, and the viewer knows what is there, but the distinct features are no longer discernable. It has merged with a larger whole.

Studying New York is a similar experience. The state is composed of a myriad of locations, ranging from rural regions as diverse as eastern Long Island and the Adirondacks to towns and city wards, each with its own history. Yet as one steps back certain regularities emerge and New York comes to life as a vital, dynamic entity. Back off a bit further and the state becomes part of a region that is in turn distinct within the contours of American history as a whole. As one leaves the "gallery", New York merges with the outlines of the "museum," perhaps, in this instance, the dramatic economic and demographic changes that have transformed the western world over the last two centuries.

Nonetheless, New York exists and is worth close inspection. Our picture of it, however, is incomplete. Parts of the canvas have only been sketched in, and others remain bare. The essays here add some exciting new brush strokes and colors, and will, if all goes according to plan, encourage at least a few of the "viewers" to pick up their own paints to add to the design.

THE "NEW" NEW YORK: AN
EXPANDING STATE IN THE NEW NATION

MARY-JO KLINE

The papers delivered at this conference will examine various aspects of the phenomenon that I call the "new" New York State—the physical and political unit that came into existence at the same time that our state had to learn to function as a part of the "new" nation to which it belonged. Siles and Meinig will present the results of their own painstaking research into areas of this neglected topic. For my part, I shall justify my label of "new " for the state in this period, and I shall suggest some aspects of the state's development that deserve closer study.

To be sure, a "New York" of white settlers of European blood had existed for more than 150 years before the close of the American Revolution. But in the years after 1783, there was an abrupt change in the realities of the unit over which Governor George Clinton and his successors presided. On the one hand, that reality was now limited and defined. New York's claims in the distant West, never as serious as those of such colonies as Virginia, had been put to rest. Hopes for New York's sovereignty over the Hampshire grants faded in the face of an independent government in Vermont. But, between those "lost" dreams of lands beyond the Great Lakes and of those in the Green Mountains lay a New York far vaster than any that colonial governors or patriot leaders of the Revolution had had to govern.

The white New Yorkers who cast their votes for George Clinton in 1777 lived in strips of territory that covered less than 10,000 square miles. The state that Clinton had to govern in peacetime encompassed nearly 50,000 square miles. Before the Revolution, white settlement was confined to Long Island and Manhattan, to the Hudson Valley, to a few scattered settlements north of Albany and west a hundred miles along the Mohawk, and to brave outposts on the Upper Susquehanna. Beyond these settlements lived the Iroquois, whose rights to their lands were protected by the British crown. Traditionally, New York's frontiers had been a financial and emotional burden for the colony and the young state—a region whose defense drained men and money. But after the Revolution, New York's frontiers became a potential source of wealth and strength. The wilderness was there to be exploited, not merely to be defended.

There were, of course, conflicting claims to this wilderness empire, and settlement of these disputes was one of the first orders of business for George Clinton's administration at the close of the Revolution. Before New York could realize any profits from the sale of these public lands or could welcome settlers to its frontier, the state had to be able to promise clear title to the tracts that it offered. Two groups stood in the way of such title.

First, of course, there were the New York Iroquois. Little attention was given to the rights of such tribes as the Mohawks, who had joined the British during the Revolution. The Treaty of Paris contained no provision for the security of the lands of the Crown's former Indian allies, and such "Loyalist" tribes could expect to find few defenders. Indeed, as early as 1782 New York had proclaimed its right to dispose of Mohawk lands when Clintion set asside the "Military Tract" for veterans of the Revolution. However, the rights of tribes that had sided with the patriot cause or who had remained neutral during the Revolution could not be so easily ignored.

Nor could Clinton overlook the claims of the commonwealth of Massachusetts. As a colony, Massachusetts had claimed a substantial part of western New York beyond the Hudson on the basis of its provincial "sea-to-sea" charter. As a state, Massachusetts revived these claims in 1784, and the Continental Congress appointed a special commission to reconcile the dispute.

Clinton did not wait for settlement of the dispute with Massachusetts before he set to work to obtain land cessions from New York's Indians. In short order, he proclaimed New York's right to treat with its resident tribes, and the weak national government under the Articles of Confederation turned its back on its responsibilities to these nations. The business of obtaining the Indians' lands for New York State began at Fort Herkimer in 1785, when the Oneidas and Tuscaroras ceded their tribal lands between the Chenango and Unadilla rivers.

The following year, New York and Massachusetts concluded an agreement that gave New York political sovereignty over all of the western part of the state. In return, Massachusetts received physical ownership of some six million acres in western New York beyond the "Preemption Line," which ran from Sodus Bay on Lake Ontario south through Seneca Lake to the Pennsylvania boundary, as well as a smaller tract near modern Owego, where Massachusetts speculators had invested in the "Boston Ten Townships." Beyond the Preemption Line, Massachusetts had the sole right to win cessions from resident Indians. To the east, New York had a free hand. In treaties signed at Fort Schuyler in September 1788, Clinton and his Indian commissioners obtained cessions of the remaining lands of the Oneidas and the Onondagas (barring small reservations). A similar treaty with the Cayugas came five months later.

The story of Massachusetts's "preemption" lands was infinitely more complicated. Hard pressed for cash, Massachusetts sold its rights to a syndicate headed by Oliver Phelps and Nathaniel Gorham in 1788. That same year Phelps obtained cessions from the Indians to two-thirds of the tract. However, Phelps and Gorham were unable to meet their financial obligations to Massachusetts, and title to the Phelps-Gorham Purchase soon passed on to Robert Morris, the Philadelphia merchant and "Financier" of the Revolution. Of this tract, Morris conveyed most of the section east of the Genesee to the associates of the British magnate, Sir William Pulteney. West of the Genesee, the bulk of the land was sold to a syndicate of Amsterdam bankers who became known as the Holland Land Company.[1]

Although the last Indian rights to these lands were not surrendered until 1798, most of the "new" New York was cleared for sale to white settlers by 1789, the year in which the federal government was inaugurated in New York City. The state of New York was then faced with the challenge of establishing political and economic sovereignty over a territory that, in fact as well as in inked lines on parchment maps, stretched to the St. Lawrence on the north and to the Great Lakes on the west. And the challenge had to be met simultaneously with making the "new" state itself part of a new national government. The challenge of making this unsettled frontier function as part of the eleventh state of the new Union was great—so great that it may have colored the development of New York down to the present day.

It was not merely the extent of this territory but its physical nature that posed special challenges for those who would make the "new" New York operate as a unit. Northern and western New York was blessed with abundant rivers and magnificent lakes. But, with the exception of the Mohawk, these waterways stubbornly flowed in directions that did not serve the purposes of New York statemen, speculators, and merchants. Even the Mohawk was a mixed blessing. Although its valley offered a convenient land passage for New Englanders eager to claim cheap lands in the New York interior, the river itself was so clogged with glacial refuse in the form of boulders and rapids that much of its course was impassable by any craft but Indian canoes. And the Mohawk's junction with the Hudson was blocked by the Cohoes Falls.

---

1. For a summary of Clinton's Indian policy, see Barbara Graymont, "New York State Indian Policy after the Revolution," *New York History* 57 (1976), 438-474. For the details of the transfers of Massachusetts's preemption rights, see Barbara A. Chernow, *Robert Morris: Land Speculator, 1790-1801* (New York, 1978), Chapter II.

Once settlers moved from the Mohawk Valley, the state's geographical and topographical dilemma became even more apparent. To the north, rivers on the eastern slopes of the Adirondacks flowed into Lake Champlain, which, in turn flowed to the St. Lawrence and Canadian ports. Western Adirondack streams were no more obliging—their waters went to Lake Ontario and the St. Lawrence. The western and southern slopes of the Catskills fed the commerce of Baltimore and Philadelphia, not Albany and New York City. Further west, the rich valleys of the Tioga and the Chemung were also part of the Susquehanna watershed. The Genesee region was alluvial tributary of Lake Ontario, while the state's southwestern corner was drained by tributaries of the Allegheny, which swelled the trade of Pittsburgh in neighboring Pennsylvania.

More than forty years ago, Oliver W. Holmes pointed out that New York's transportation porblems were minor so long as settlement was confined to the Hudson and eastern Mohawk Valleys. Indeed, he remarked that "many conditions of the true frontier were scarcely known along the Hudson because the river made travel to and from the metropolis easy and common."[2] In the "new" New York of the 1780's and the 1790's, settlers would get a full taste of the "true frontier." The region's physical nature made such an experience inevitable.

Yet, in 1856, Horatio Seymour boasted of the *benefits* that the state's geography had brought to New York. "The waters which drain from our territories," Seymour proclaimed, "flow by the principal commercial cities of the Union.... Thus our State enjoys the apparently inconsistent advantages of having the deepest channels of commerce with the west, and at the same time, of being at the head of the great valleys of the United States.... It enables us to penetrate with our Canals and Railroads into all parts of the country by following the easy and natural routes of rivers. We

---

2. Oliver W. Holmes, "The Turnpike Era," Alexander C. Flick, ed., *History of the State of New York*, vol. 5 (*Conquering the Wilderness*, Albany, 1934), 257.

can go into twenty States, and into two-thirds of the territories of the Union, without leaving the courses of
valleys."[3]

The process by which New York turned the "wrong direction" of its rivers to the state's advantage was not a simple
one. And because the Erie Canal and the era that it inaugurated marked the triumph of this process, historians
have tended to slight any of the state's efforts to create a
transportation system that cannot be conveniently labeled as
forbear of the canals. Historians routinely discuss Sir Henry
Moore's pre-Revolutionary suggestion for clearing the
Mohawk, Christopher Colles's plans of the 1780's for a canal
along that valley, and Philip Schuyler's Inland Lock Navigation Companies.[4] But Moore's and Colles's schemes were
never put into effect. Schuyler and his associates failed in
their attempts to improve navigation on the Mohawk. In
comparison to the attention given to these failures, only
slight notice has been given to New York's far more successful program to provide its citizens in the North and the
West with land carriage.

The state's attempts to give its frontiers roads began
almost as soon as Indian lands east of the Preemption Line
had been ceded to the state. An historian of road-building in
the Mid-Atlantic region found that New York had a
"definite state aid policy" for its roads and highways by the
end of 1790. For the next thirty-five years, until canals provided a more effective solution to the state's transportation
problem, this program continued. Although the "turnpike"
era of this policy has been studied,[5] the earlier phase, in

---

3. Horatio Seymour, *A Lecture on the Topography and History of New-York*
(Utica, 1856), 809.
4. The literature on New York canals is too vast to be summarized here. For a
brief account of the canal's precursors, see Julius Rubin, "An Innovating Public
Improvement: The Erie Canal," Carter Goodrich, et al., *Canals and American
Economic Development* (New York, 1961), 15-66.
5. This attitude is reflected in the focus on turnpikes in the Holmes study cited
above and in Joseph Durrenberger, *Turnpikes: A Study of the Toll Road Movement in the Middle Atlantic States and Maryland* (Valdosta, Ga., 1931).

which state action, not private investment, financed these roads, has been given little notice. And the motives behind this government policy have never been adequately analysed.

New Yorkers felt a special sense of urgency in dealing with the problem of providing transportation for their frontier. This does not seem to have arisen from any fear of political loss of the new territory. True, Virginia had lost its frontier counties in Kentucky to separatist demands. But secessionist movements in western New York were apparently confined to John Livingston's half-hearted attempt of 1793 to erect a new state in the region in order to secure his claims under leases negotiated with the Iroquois.[6] Still, in an era when farmers relied on water carriage, there was good reason to fear that the region might be lost to the state in economic and commercial terms.

In calling for an ever more forceful and systematic program for the development of frontier transportation in January 1791, George Clinton reminded the state legislature that the frontiers were now "freed from apprehensions of danger" from Indian attack and were "rapidly increasing and must soon yield extensive resources for profitable commerce; this consideration forcibly recommends the policy of continuing to facilitate the means of communication with them, as well to strengthen the bands of society, as to prevent the produce of those fertile districts from being diverted to other markets."[7]

Three months later, William Cooper put the matter more succinctly, if less elegantly, when he wrote to Attorney General Aaron Burr to urge implementation of a new state law for construction of a road from the south end of Otsego Lake to the Mohawk. Cooper pointed out that the petition for such a road was "by way of counteracting the maneuvers of the merchants of Philadelphia who have been active to

---

6. Julian P. Boyd, "Attempts to Form New States in New York and Pennsylvania," *New York History.*, 12 (1931), 257-270.
7. Charles Z. Lincoln, ed., *Messages from the Governors* [of New York State] . . . (11 vols., Albany, 1909), 2:311-312.

Secure the trade of this western Country to their City."[8]

As every historian of the period has pointed out, the eagerness of investors in western lands for frontier roads was tied directly to their need for settlers in the tracts in which they had invested. But they were not alone in their concern. New Yorkers were not ready to heed David Hume's warnings against the "Jealousy of Trade." Indeed, few Americans of the time took seriously that philosopher's assurances that no state need "entertain apparehensions, that their neighbours will improve to such a degree in every art and manufacture, as to have no demand from them." New Yorkers had to look no further than New Jersy to see the fate of a state whose commerce became tributary to its neighbors. Merchants of New York City and of ports on the Hudson were as eager for manmade routes that would bring them the frontier trade as were the land speculators who saw those roads as avenues that would take prospective purchasers to their tracts. And New Yorkers were scarcely alone in their "jealousy" of their own trade—Philadelphia merchants fought for roads that would secure that commonwealth's frontier trade to their city, and Louis Hartz has commented at length on the sense of interstate commercial rivalry that persisted in Pennsylvania well into the nineteenth century.[9]

However, there was more than state chauvinism behind the sense of urgency with which eighteenth century businessmen viewed the trade patterns of newly settled regions. When Christopher Colles presented his plan for improvement of the Mohawk to the New York legislature in the 1780's, he warned, "[I]t is an indisputable fact, that trade is like water, when it once passes in any particular channel, it is not easily diverted or drawn away into another."[10] In the

---

8. Letter of April 4, 1790, New York Historical Society: Cooper.
9. Wilbur C. Plummer, *The Road Policy of Pennsylvania* (Philadelphia, 1925); Louis Hartz, *Economic Policy and Democratic Thought: Pennsylvania, 1776-1860* (Cambridge, Mass., 1948), 9-17.
10. Christopher Colles, *Proposals for the speedy Settlement of the Waste and Unappropriated Lands on the Western Frontier of the State of New-York* (New York, 1785), 13.

1790's and early 1800's, most Americans still shared this notion that trade routes established early in a society's existence were likely to prevail through custom and habit. Warnings that the state's northern and western trade might be *permanently* lost to other states—or to Canada—unless prompt action were taken persist in writings on the improvement of land and water routes in New York down to the Erie Canal era.[11]

The Erie Canal not only offered a lasting solution to the problems of transportation in the "new" New York, but it also proved that habits of trade could be changed when man offered clearly more efficient routes than nature had provided. However, the Canal was the end of a movement, not an isolated phenomenon, and its triumph only underscores the need to know more about New York's earlier attempts to tie together the "new" state.

First, the roads constructed in New York after 1789 were at least a partial success, unlike the abortive attempts to improve waterways in the 1790's. By 1800, when Charles Williamson urged construction of a new turnpike through the Southern Tier from the Genesee to the Hudson, he was obliged to anticipate the protests of Albany merchants who had hitherto enjoyed a near monopoly of the Geneses trade thanks to earlier roads built in the north.[12] In a decade of public road-building, New York managed to generate enough commerce along these highways to make the location of additional roads the subject of competition between Albany on the one hand and trading towns like Catskill and Kingston further south on the Hudson.[13]

---

11. For examples, see [Charles Williamson], *Observations on the Proposed State Road from Hudson's River, near the City of Hudson, to Lake Erie, by the Oleout* . . . (New York, 1816); [DeWitt Clinton], *Memorial of the Citizens of New-York, in favour of a Canal Navigation between the Great Western Lakes and the tide-water of the Hudson* (New York, 1816); Gideon Granger *Speech delivered before a Convention of the People of Ontario, Co., N.Y., Jan. 8, 1817* . . . (Canandaigua, 1817).

12. Williamson, *loc. cit.*

13. Here I must qualify my own claim. The early state roads had this effect in the opinion of contemporary observers. No historian has taken the time to verify the supposed impact of these roads on the towns along their routes.

Perhaps more significant in judging the success of the state roads and turnpikes was the opinion of New York's neighbor and commercial rival to the south. Pennsylvanians recognized the impact of that construction program and reacted to it strongly. By the War of 1812, New York boasted turnpikes 324 miles long. It led the nation not only in investing in turnpikes but in constucting them.[14] When plans were heard for federal support of a Great Lakes–Atlantic canal in 1811, William J. Duane warned his fellow Pennsylvanians that New York's enviable record in making internal improvements might well persuade the United States government that any such canal should lie within New York. "Our negligence," Duane complained, "has been mistaken for inability."[15]

Federal aid for a Great Lakes canal did not come, of course. But it was New York, not Pennsylvania, that went ahead to build such a waterway at state expense. New York established itself as an innovator in internal improvements. Pennsylvania contented itself with being an imitator. In 1811, following construction of the Cumberland Road, the Pennsylvania legislature responded with a burst of bills for internal improvements. Once New York began construction of the Erie Canal, Pennsylvania reacted with another such flurry of activity. And it was only when the Erie Canal was near completion in 1823 that Pennsylvania began to pass canal acts of its own in earnest.[16]

In a comparative study of road construction in the mid-Atlantic region, Joseph Durrenberger suggested that New

---

14. Durrenberger, *op. cit.*, 62.

15. William J. Duane, *Letters Addressed to the people of Pennsylvania respecting the internal improvement of the Commonwealth by means of Roads and Canals* (Philadelphia, 1811), 53.

16. J. Lee Hartman, "Pennsylvania's Grand Plan of Post-Revolutionary Internal Improvement," *Pennsylvania Magazine*, 65 (1941), 439-457; William G. Gephart, *Transportation and Industrial Development in the Middle West* (New York, 1909), 117-118; Durrenberger, *op. cit.*, p. 50; Willard R. Rhoads, "The Pennsylvania Canal," *Western Pennsylvania History Magazine*, 43 (1960), 207; William A. Russ, Jr., "The Partnership between Public and Private Initiative in the History of Pennsylvania," *Pennsylvania History*, 20 (1953), 7-8.

York's successful and innovative program may have arisen from the fact that New York's needs were greater than Pennsylvania's. In New York, ordinary resources and conventional measures would not meet the peculiar demands that the "new" state placed on an old transportation system.[17] Nathan Miller's findings of persistent "mercantilist" attitudes in New York long after the colonial era[18] are quite understandable when we consider the scope of the problems presented by the "new" state—problems that could not be met by laissez-faire policies or by "natural" development. It is interesting to speculate that it was the very inconvenient and cumbersome pattern of the topography of western and northern New York that forced the state to adopt measures that not only met those physical problems but also set the stage for New York's emergence as an "Empire" state after the opening of the Erie Canal.[19]

But an "empire" is something more than roads and canals. It is a political system as well, and we can not afford to ignore the implications of the state's "newness" in fashioning and refashioning politics and government. Historians of New York's political parties have been more ready than specialists in other fields to give due attention to the implications of territorial expansion on the state as a whole, but the beginnings of such a detailed and systematic analysis of the phenomenon are comparatively recent. Only thirty years ago, so responsible a scholar as David Ellis could repeat generalizations concerning the Republican influence of "the first generation of New Englanders" in New York who "tended to join in the fight for democracy."[20] Thanks to two studies completed only in the last fifteen years, we now know that the political effects of New York's expanding frontier on

---

17. Durrenberger, *op. cit.*, p. 59.
18. Nathan Miller, *The Enterprise of a Free People: Aspects of Economic Development in New York State during the Canal Period, 1792-1838* (Ithaca, N.Y., 1962), 3-19.
19. For the evolution of New York's "empire" status, see David M. Ellis, "Rise of the Empire State, 1790-1820," *New York History,* 56 (1975), 5-27.
20. "The Yankee Invasion of New York, 1783-1850," *ibid.,* 32 (1951): 3-17.

its settlers and of those frontiersmen on the state were far more subtle and far-reaching than any supposed influx of New England egalitarians.

The first of these studies was Alfred Young's *The Democratic Republicans of New York: The Origins, 1763-1797,* published in 1967. The second study, less well known, is a doctoral dissertation accepted at Columbia University only two years ago, Dominick D. DeLorenzo's "The New York Federalists: Forces of Order."[21] I am sure that neither gentleman would be insulted if I suggest that many of their findings are tentative. Like any statewide surveys, they require the support of detailed studies at the local level—studies that have not been done. But both historians agree on the critical impact of New York's expansion in terms of territory and of population upon the state's political development in the early national period.

Some of the results of expansion that these studies detail were predictable. By 1800, the number of counties in the state had tripled. Almost all of these new jurisdictions were carved from what had been "Montgomery County" in 1784—a subdivision that comprised all of the state north and west of Albany. Each new county, of course, gave additional sources of patronage to the Council of Appointment. There was a clear relationship between the multiplication of county governments and the bitter rivalry between governor and state senators for control of the power of nomination on that council. Even more important, the state constitution of 1777 had provided for septennial censuses to be followed by mandatory legislative reapportionment. Changes in the regional balance of political power in the state were preordained and non-negotiable.

However, the recent studies by Young and De Lorenzo go far beyond such obvious influences of expansion on the New York body politic. Each focuses considerable attention on the

---

21. Alfred F. Young, *The Democratic Republicans of New York: The Origins, 1763-1797* (Chapel Hill, N.C., 1967); Dominick D. De Lorenzo, "The New York Federalists: Forces of Order," Doctoral Dissertation, Columbia University, 1979.

failure of the Federalist party to retain control of the west in New York. Young's study, which closes in 1797, suggests some of the reasons for the apparent paradox of "frontier Federalism" in the early 1790s as well as the reasons for its ultimate failure. He points out that, far from importing Republican tendencies to their adopted state, New England settlers in the 1780s and early 1790s brought along their native New England Federalism. Domination of many frontier sections by Federalist landlords strengthened this prediliction, and Federalist control of the national government confirmed this bias so long as defense was a major concern for the frontier. However, Young sees the Federalists as the "victims of their own success" after 1795. Jay's Treaty ended the occupation of the posts at Oswego and Niagara, and defense was no longer a paramount concern for the region. Landlords and resident speculators like William Cooper overstepped the bounds allowed even by contemporary standards of "deference" and lost much of their influence. And John Jay's election as governor in 1795 deprived the Federalists of a convenient political whipping boy in the august person of George Clinton.[22]

DeLorenzo's dissertation carries the story to 1800, with a concluding chapter summarizing trends in the state to 1816. He places responsibility for the Federalist party's demise in New York squarely on the shoulders of Federalist leaders themselves. According to DeLorenzo, these men, beginning with John Jay, failed to respond to the demands of New York's frontier and semi-frontier counties. Only an "upstate Hamilton," in De Lorenzo's words, could have rescued the Federalists from their fate.[23]

Wherever the fault lay, the "new" New York discarded Federalist leadership. What Young called "a quiet revolution"[24] dictated that those northern and western counties must be heard. In 1796 New York reapportioned legislative seats on the basis of the first state census that reflected the

---

22. Young, *op. cit.,* Chapter 12, *passim* and 496-497.
23. "New York Federalists," 197-198, 261.

impact of the new frontier expansion. Each succeeding enumeration meant more legislative seats for the "new" regions of the state. And, as both Young and DeLorenzo note in detail, the state's property requirements for voters gave the west a disproportionate influence in state elections as that region boasted a far higher percentage of L100 freeholders than older counties.[24]

Still, Young's and DeLorenzo's studies only begin to sketch the picture. Did the Federalist party lose New York because of its own failings or did the Republican party "coopt" frontier issues for its own use? These questions cannot be answered without examining party history into the nineteenth century. We cannot treat the state Federalist party's history after 1800 as a mere postscript to the election of Thomas Jefferson.

As late as 1804 Gideon Granger sensed a real danger that Federalists could exploit sectional interests in New York. Granger, then Jefferson's postmaster general, was one of the ablest political reporters of his day, and his warnings cannot be taken lightly. In a letter to DeWitt Clinton, Granger pointed to the threats posed by Aaron Burr's rumored attempts to woo both frontier leaders and the "New England Interest" in his 1804 bid for the governorship. "The political ballance of your State," Granger lectured Clinton," is to be decided by the ten Western Counties who are principally Yankees, and who if I mistake not, will go with New England whenever her Citizens are agreed among themselves."[25]

Republicans, like the Federalists in the 1790s, could become the victims of their own diplomatic successes. The Louisiana Purchase had removed the threat of foreign attack from the West. Frontiersmen would no longer give automatic support to the party in power in Washington because of their need for defense. "Before the late Treaty," Granger wrote Clinton, "the greatest object of the western people was safety

---

24. Young, *op. cit.*, 507.
25. *Ibid.* 585-588; "New York Federalists," 240-241.

now it is prosperity." Granger even predicted a new nation-wide sectional alliance that could threaten the Jeffersonian party. "When they [the westerners] look abroad to the various States in the Union, they must perceive that they can-not derive any aid from the Atlantic States South of the Sus-quehannah—neither Merchants—Capitol—Carriers—pur-chasers—artists—mechanics—nor indeed Settlers . . . ."

Granger foresaw that "the period is not remote when a strong political union is formed between the States east of the Delaware & west of the mountains. It is founded in nature. It cannot be successfully resisted."[26] In 1804, Burr, a veteran of New York's political wars, seemed ready to capitalize on this phenomenon at the local level, but this "whiggish" junction of western and eastern interests failed to materialize in New York in 1804. A dozen years later, it did appear in the fight over state construction of the Erie Canal, but in 1816 and 1817, the matter became a regional and not a partisan bone of contention. Northern and western counties allied with mercantile interests in New York City in their fight for funds for the canal. Counties whose economic interests and geographic locations gave them no obvious stake in the matter (Long Island and the Hudson Valley counties) opposed the scheme.[27]

Surely there was no better symbol of the bipartisan nature of the coalition behind the Erie Canal than the choice of the two New Yorkers who went to Washington to plead the case for federal construction of the waterway—DeWitt Clinton and Gouverneur Morris. The nephew of George Clinton made the journey in the enthusiastic company of New York's highest (perhaps its most ultramontane) Federalist—the two joined by their personal speculations in New York frontier lands and their commitment to a Great Lakes canal. The ex-planation of this marvelous nonpartisan partnership awaits further study. Can we say that it was the result of Federalist

---

26. Granger to Clinton, March 27, 1804, Special Collections, Columbia University: Clinton Papers.
27. Julius Rubin, *loc. cit.,* 57.

ineptitude in not exploiting the canal issue? Was it a tribute to DeWitt Clinton's political skills? Or was it, instead, a reflection of the fact that the problems created by the "new" New York were so great that old loyalties and allegiances were put aside?

But there are "political" issues beyond party structure and electoral failure and success to be studied in this era. We do not know, for instance, whether New Yorkers deliberately attempted to give their "new" counties a sense of partnership with the old—whether there was a conscious concern for implanting a sense of "state" citizenship in New York's new counties and their residents. As late as 1817, Gideon Granger (by then a resident of western New York) argued for construction of the Erie Canal to "maintain the unity of the state—dissipate every fear of a division."[28] Was this mere window-dressing, or did Granger voice a common and persistent concern among New Yorkers as they watched settlement in their state expand to the north and west?

An investigation of "old" New Yorkers' contemporary attitudes towards their own frontier would be especially fruitful where the state's Federalists are concerned. Here, research may offer us a case study of party theory versus party practice. We are now too sophisticated to dismiss the anti-western expressions of New York Federalists like John Jay and Gouverneur Morris as reflections of nothing but sectional bias, but we have yet to examine their behavior when confronted with a frontier close at hand.[29]

Dominick DeLorenzo has suggested that some underlying philosophical attitudes of the Federalists made it impossible for them to deal with the demands of the "new" New York. There was, he writes, an "inherent instability of popular

---

28. Granger, *Speech delivered . . . Jan. 8, 1817.*
29. For attempts to explain the anti-frontier bias of eastern conservatives in the Confederation era, see Paul C. Phillips, "American Opinions regarding the West, 1778-1783," Mississippi Valley Historical Association, *Proceedings,* 7 (1913-1914), 291-293; and Francis S. Philbrick's "Introduction" to Illinois State Historical Library, *Collections,* 25 ("The Laws of the Illinois Territory, 1809-1818," Springfield, 1950), cclxxiv.

government [that] was simply magnified by the unpredic-
tability of the election process in areas of new settlement or in
those featuring transient populations,"[30] and that Federalist
leaders could not deal with such unstable factors. However,
De Lorenzo is too scrupulous a scholar to use Jay's failure to
"keep" the frontier for Federalism during his governorship
as proof of this theory. He admits that Jay's ineptness as an
executive was as great a cause as any other of Federalist ero-
sion on the New York frontier in these years.

And as for Morris, as eloquent a spokesman as one could
wish for those frightened by the notion of expansion into the
wilderness, we have no serious studies at all. This despite the
fact that on Morris's return to America in 1798 after a decade
abroad, he began a career as land developer in the St.
Lawrence Valley and as an apostle of a Great Lakes canal.
Surely this phase of Morris's life deserves examination in
terms of its explication of his views on how a frontier should
be won—how a wilderness might be subdued in a proper
and "respectable" Federalist manner.

Concern for creating a productive and "proper" frontier is
easy to find in this period. An anonymous pamphleteer of
1810 hinted darkly at the evils to be expected if settlers were
left to their own devices without proper supervision—and,
not incidentally, without a Great Lakes canal: "We know
that people who live far from markets, and cannot sell their
produce, naturally become indolent and vicious. Having little to do, they do less . . . There are people in the western
country, settled on a bountiful soil, who do not raise a bushel
of grain except what is eaten by the family, or what is made
in Whiskey, for the purpose of drowning thought and
destroying soul and body."[31]

Still, with all these good reasons for studying the history of
the "new" New York, William Siles is justified in calling this
period the "dark ages" in the writing the history of New
York. (Indeed, studies of northern New York for the years

---

30. "New York Federalists," 197.
31. *Observations on Canal Navigation* (n.p., 1818), 11.

before completion of the Erie Canal are so sparse that "stone ages" might be a more appropriate term for that region's historiography.) We do not, for instance, even know where the New York frontier line lay during the decades of the state's expansion.[32]

However, the first forty years of the "new" New York, 1784 to 1824, are less dark than they once were. In the last three decades, the comparative neglect of many aspects of the region's history has come to an end with town and county studies, monographs on state Indian policy, and sophisticated biographies of some of the state's great land developers and speculators.[33] There are, of course, regions and sub-regions in the state's history that represent virgin soil for the demographer, the political analyst, the statistician, and even the journeyman "generalist" historian. We have always had rich sources for investigating the impact of New York's "newness" after 1784, and we now have sources that are "new" to our generation in terms of accessibility to scholars. The records of the Holland Land Company in Amsterdam are now available on microfilm. County and local historical records are being assembled, and this trend is best typified by the recent publication of the microfilm reels of the "Burned-Over District" Project, which has collected for our ease the archives of dozens of religious groups on the New York frontier.

While this paper clearly betrays my own bias for economic and political history, social historians have equally great

---

32. The last scholar to attempt to map this line was Ruth Higgins in an appendix to *Expansion in New York with especial Reference to the Eighteenth Century* (Columbus, Ohio, 1931). Higgins tried to approximate this bound for the 1790s by drawing a line that followed the first known white settlement in places that later became towns. This produced a map that shows the New York "frontier"; several miles west of Rochester in 1791.

33. The works referred to here include Chernow's *Robert Morris;* William Chazanof's *Joseph Ellicott and the Holland Land Company* (Syracuse, 1970); Neill McNall's *An Agricultural History of the Genesee Valley, 1790-1860* (Philadelphia, 1952); Barbara Graymont's *The Iroquois in the American Revolution* (Syracuse, 1972); and James Frost's *Life on the Upper Susquehanna, 1783-1860* (New York, 1951).

cause for complaint about the quality of past work in the "new" New York—and equally good reason for rejoicing about opportunities for future research. Each group of archives that has been catalogued and microfilmed will aid them as well. And specialists in all fields have the benefit of a convenient research "control" in the experience of our neighbors in Pennsylvania. Of course, that commonwealth's experience was not identical to New York's. On the one hand, Pennsylvanians had carved out permanent settlements on their southwestern and western frontiers before the Revolution. On the other, Indian warfare delayed fullscale opening of unsettled public lands in Pennsylvania until the mid 1790s. But enough analogies exist to allow fruitful comparisons.

Meinig's paper, for instance, will offer evidence that New York and Pennsylvania became part of a special region of development during the first years of the new republic. Continuing analysis of demographic patterns of economic and cultural "exchange" between New York and her neighbors may provide us with one of the most exciting areas of interdisciplinary research in the next decades. And these studies may lead a new generation of scholars to rediscover David Ellis's twenty-seven-year old call for regional studies of the Mid Atlantic states. When Ellis advanced this notion in 1954, his critics argued that New York was not part of a "classical," easily defined "region."[34] And, of course, it is not. It was a hallmark of the "new" New York that the state and its citizens remade their economic "region" while settlers from other states and other nations constantly changed the cultural "region" of which New York was a part. And this fact brings us to the best argument that we have for an examination of the "new" state.

It may be a tribute to our heritage from another of our cultural partners in this era—New England—that I feel call-

34. Ellis, "New York and Middle Atlantic Regionalism," *New York History*, 35 (1954), 3-13, and the rejoinder, "Middle Atlantic Regionalism Revisited," *ibid.*, 36 (1955, 413-421.

ed upon to advance a broader, moral justification for pursuing the study of New York's frontier history. Historians of our state feel periodically obliged to announce compelling philosophical reasons for pursuing work that, in fact, they thoroughly enjoy. And the reason which is presented most frequently is Frederick Jackson Turner's plea that American historians look to the history of the Mid Atlantic states for the roots of the distinctive traits that he had found in the rural West.

In 1972 Milton Klein pursued this theme in his essay, "New York in the American Colonies: A New Look." Recalling Turner's comment that the Mid Atlantic states were the most "typically American" of the nation's older regions, Klein argued forcefully for a closer study of the origins of that Americanism in New York. Regarding partisan politics, Klein wrote: "By 1775, New Yorkers were accustomed to what the country would become adept in during the years ahead."[35] If we alter Klein's terminal date to 1820 and broaden his statement to include all aspects of the state's experience, we may find a clue to the "Americanism" that Turner sensed in New York.

Like the states of the American West, the "new" New York met the challenge of peopling its unsettled territories within the framework of a federal system. It integrated new voters on the frontier into local parties that were part of a developing national political system. Unlike states in which expansion had taken place during the colonial era, frontier New Yorkers—like farmers of Indiana and Texas and Michigan—could seek favors from a national government. The Paxton Boys of provincial Pennsylvania had no choice but to march on Philadelphia. Farmers and merchants of western and northern New York could present their demands to Albany and to Washington. And Congressmen from frontier regions were free to make alliances with legislators from other states in pursuit of their mutual goals.

---

35. *New York History*, 53 (1972), 138-139.

Like her sisters beyond the Appalachians and the Mississippi, New York was forced to create an economic system for an area whose "paper" boundaries bore little relationship to natural topography or to the patterns of trade dictated by unimproved mountains and waterways. New York, like the West, had to invent machines and methods that would overcome such geographical handicaps. In the process, New York became part of a national economy, thanks to the success of its own innovations in transportation and marketing.

Again like those newer members of the Union, New York welcomed a wide range of ethnic and religious groups to its advancing frontier. And somehow there emerged from this process a distinct image of the "Yorker" and the society in which he lived—just as "Hoosiers" and "Buckeyes" created such self-images in later decades.

In the past, the possibility that New York's expansion might teach us something about the broader history of the American frontier has been ignored because it was assumed that New York's pattern of landlords, speculators, and developers posed too sharp a contrast to the supposedly "free" nature of settlement in the West. However, Siles's paper will explore the possibility that, in reality, the experience of New York was far closer to that of the West than our traditional myths would have us believe.

Once legends are put aside—the legends of professional historical scholarship as well as the legends of laymen—the study of the "new" New York may finally come into its own. We should not feel too guilty for having neglected the "newness" of New York so long. Even New Yorkers of the Confederation era ignored this obvious fact. After all, Abraham Lansing and Robert Yates, New York Antifederalist delegates to the Philadelphia Convention, blithely allied themselves with the "small states" in that assembly.[36]

With two hundred years' additional hindsight, we can do better than Lansing and Yates. And the study of the "new"

---

36. This point is explored by DeLorenzo, "New York Federalists," 190.

New York may prove to be almost as exciting as was the process by which native New Yorkers, European immigrants, and settlers from New England and Pennsylvania turned the sprawling mass of misplaced mountains and misdirected rivers into an Empire State. Should any of the papers presented at this conference persuade others to join us in such research, I can do no better than to recall Aaron Burr's advice to a young Westchester politician in 1832. I wish any converts to our cause "a great deal of fun and honor & profit during the campaign."[37]

---

37. Burr to Aaron Ward, January 14, 1832, Boston Public Library.

PIONEERING IN THE GENESEE COUNTRY :

ENTREPRENEURIAL STRATEGY AND

THE CONCEPT OF A CENTRAL PLACE

WILLIAM H. SILES

Scholars of American westward expansion have generally been aware of the role land companies and land speculators played in opening up wilderness land to pioneer settlement. Scholars of New York State history are certainly aware of the Phelps-Gorham Land Company and its pioneering operation in central New York after 1788. Yet available literature on the subject of upstate New York speculation indicates that while scholars have understood the scope of this operation, they have not yet come to grips with the essence of these pioneering practices and the pattern within which these practices are related to other processes of settlement.[1]

Since the mid-1970's, new ways of viewing land company and pioneering operations have emerged from basic research done on several geographic areas in different periods of time. Out of these new studies has come a new understanding of the pioneering process. The new view holds that land companies, land operators, and individual settlers shared a common estimation of the wilderness as a commodity to be ex-

---

1. See, for example, Ruth L. Higgins, *Expansion in New York* (Columbus, 1931); Lois Kimball Mathews. *The Expansion of New England* (New York, 1909); Arthur C. Parker, *Charles Williamson: Builder of the Genesee Country* (Rochester, 1927); Paul D. Evans, *The Holland Land Company* (Buffalo, 1924). On the topic of land speculation, ground breaking articles were published by Paul Wallace Gates, "The Role of the Land Speculator in Western Development," in Paul Wallace Gates, *Landlords and Tenants on the Prairie Frontier* (Ithaca, 1973), 48-71; and, Ray Allan Billington, "Origin of the Land Speculator as a Frontier Type," *Agricultural History,* 19 (October, 1945), 204-212.

ploited, traded, leased, bought, and sold by both speculators
and settlers. The commercial nature of frontier settlement
and development is a key factor and dynamic concept ex-
plaining the steady spread of Americans and American institutions in all directions prior to and certainly after the
American Revolution.[2]

New studies have not only demonstrated how commercial
tendencies were present from the very beginning of frontier
development, they have accurately shifted the focus of frontier studies away from the activity of typical pioneering types
such as farmers and traders, trappers and drovers, to frontier
speculators, town planners and developers. It was they, it is
argued, more than farmers who had a significant impact on
the social and economic shape of large sections of the
American frontier. Town planners and town builders, working with clearly understood commercial purposes, were in
fact, the primary agents for pioneering America's wilderness
territory.[3] What scholars are now realizing is that effective
pioneering requires the stimulating of dynamic agricultural
and commercial activity with a strategically located central
place, a regular supply of new settlers, and the creation of effective links between the central place and established
markets. Successful frontier operations are always essentially

2. See James T. Lemon, *Best Poor Man's Country: A Geographical Study of Early
Southeastern Pennsylvania* (Baltimore, 1972); Carville V. Earle, *The Evolution of a
Tidewater Settlement System* (Chicago, 1975); Stephanie Grauman Wolf, *Urban
Village: Population, Community, and Family Structures in Germantown, Penn-
sylvania, 1683-1800* (Princeton, 1976); Robert D. Mitchell, *Commercialism and
Frontier: Perspectives on the Early Shenandoah Valley* (Charlottesville, 1977);
Jerome O. Steffen, *Comparative Frontiers: A Proposal for Studying the American
West* (Norman, 1980); Don Harrison Doyle, *The Social Order of a Frontier Com-
munity: Jacksonville, Illinois, 1825-1870* (Urbana, 1978); John W. Reps, *Cities of
the American West* (Princeton, 1979).

3. Reps, *op. cit.* ix-xiii; Earle, *op. cit.*, 38, 50, 63-64; Wolfe, *op. cit.*, 16, 18, 19,
25-27, 59-60, 70, 92; Mitchell, *op. cit.* xi, xiii. James T. Lemon, "Urbanization
and the Development of Eighteenth Century Southeastern Pennsylvania and Adjacent Delaware," *William and Mary Quarterly*, 3rd ser., 24 (October, 1967),
501-541; Lemon, *Best Poor Man's Country*, 49-61; W.L. Morton, "The
Significance of Site in the Settlement of the American and Canadian Wests,"
Agricultural History 3 (July, 1951), 97-104.

built upon successful commercial endeavors.

A close look at the Phelps-Gorham operation in central New York adds more evidence to support the growing concept of a constantly moving frontier dominated by nascent commercial activity. A study of the Phelps-Gorham Land Company also reveals a pattern of post-Revolutionary frontier development that may well be typical of frontier development in America. Planned towns were strategically laid out by the developers prior to settlement. These towns were then provided with institutions calculated to attract and hold settlers. The thinking on the part of the speculating company operators was to stimulate settlement and development in a specific frontier area so as to increase trade and land values in a relatively short period of time. The benefit would largely accrue to the investors, who would profit handsomely from sharply rising land values and trade.

The key factor in understanding the Phelps-Gorham speculation was their concept of centrality of settlement. This concept was more important in opening up a wilderness than settlement based solely upon land selection related to soil conditions. Discriminate settlement was valued more highly by the company than indiscriminate settlement. The land company thus demonstrated a strong interest in creating high density settlements as opposed to dispersed agricultural settlements. Centrality emphasized rapid development, specialized trades, and services, and was supposed to stimulate, in turn, rapid agricultural settlement of the hinterland. Artificially planned population centers existing in thinly settled wilderness areas would command the import trade and become the point of distribution for a very large territory. Thus, urban communities would be vanguards of settlement, and urban values, rooted in a commercial attitude toward the land, would become controlling factors in land development in upstate New York. Men of capital, rather than individual farmers were responsible for pioneering the wilderness and linking it to the settled portions of the east coast.

The post-Revolutionary pioneering process on the Phelps-

Gorham tract occurred in a region known as the Genesee
Country (from the name for that portion of a river running
between present day Avon and Mount Morris) in upstate
New York. Seneca Indians, who inhabited the region before
white settlement, called the area "Gen-nis-heo" or Beautiful
Valley, and the "Gen-ne-see' or Clear Pleasant Open
Valley.[4] The remainder of the river running from Avon
northward to Lake Ontario was known in its entirety as "Guh-
hun-da," a Large Stream.[5] The Seneca village site near Avon
became known to early white traders as "Gen-nis-heo," and
this word later became the common term for the entire river
system.[6] Still later, when a tract of land was purchased from
the Seneca by New England developers in 1788, the name
"Genesee" was applied to all the land surrendered by the
nation. After settlement began, Genesee was loosely applied
to all lands west of Utica, and all of western New York
became popularly known as the "Genesee Country."[7]

The Phelps-Gorham Purchase was the first land sale made
by the Seneca after the American Revolution. The Purchase
was a generally rectangular configuration, 43 miles wide, and
83 miles long. It was located between the Genesee River and
Seneca Lake, which marked its western and eastern boundaries, and Lake Ontario and the northern border of Pennsylvania, which marked its northern and southern boundaries. The tract contained 2,500,000 acres of land when the
Phelps-Gorham purchase was made from the Indians in
1788. It was a vast preserve of untouched natural resources,

4. George H. Harris, "Notes on the Original Terminology of the Genesee
River," Rochester Historical Society, *Publication of the Rochester Historical Society*, I (Rochester, 1892), 14. Hereafter cited as *PRHS*.
5. *Ibid.*
6. *Ibid.*
7. See the area maps in W. Pierpont White, "Indian Possessions and Settled
Areas in New York State from 1711 to 1820," Rochester Historical Society,
Publication Fund Series, VII (Rochester, 1928), 225-233. Hereafter cited as
RHSP.

capable of providing a variety of profitable returns, and was a valuable prize for ambitious land speculators, developers, colonizers, and promoters of settlement.[8]

The Phelps-Gorham Purchase

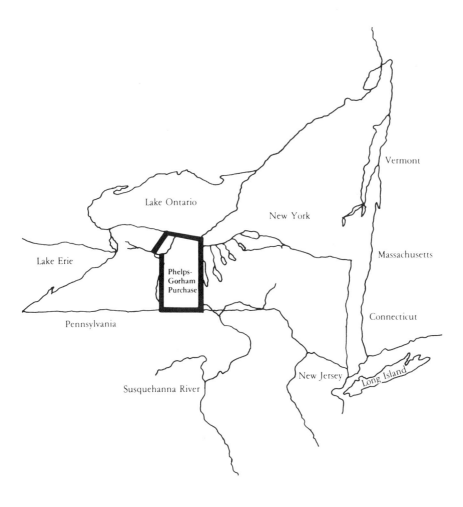

8. A map of Messrs. Gorham and Phelps Purchase, now the County of Ontario in the State of New York, *Phelps-Gorham Book of Maps,* Hubbell Papers, Princeton University, Princeton, New Jersey.

The attention of New Englanders was drawn to the
Genesee Country when Major General John Sullivan led New
England soldiers through the territory in 1779, on an expedition sent by Washington to destroy the war-making capacity
of the Indians residing in the area.[9] During their tour of du-
ty, New Englanders saw the hardwood trees, the fresh water,
the fast running streams, the abundant game, and the productive soil. Their interest was naturally awakened.[10] The
sudden collapse of the Seneca in a battle with Sullivan's army
at Newtown, New York, and their precipitious retreat to the
area around Fort Niagara, broke Seneca power over a portion
of the Genesee Country, thus making it a ripe target for
future settlement.[11] Within a relatively short period of time
after the close of the American Revolution, the real
possibilities for settlement described in the diaries of the men
in Sullivan's army became a reality.

The central question regarding Genesee Country development was who should do the developing. Was it to be
farmers or capitalists? Would access to this richly endowed
territory be given to land-short eastern families or would the
first possessors be men of wealth? The answer to this question
was decided at a conference held in Hartford, Connecticut,
between New York State and Massachusetts in 1786. What
was at stake was the establishment of state jurisdiction over
the Genesee Country. The federal government believed it
had extended its sovereignty over the general region when it
had signed a treaty with the Seneca, Mohawk, Onondaga,
and Cayuga nations at Fort Stanwix in 1784. The federal

---

9. George S. Conover (ed.), *History of Ontario Country, N.Y.* (comp. Lewis Cass
Aldrich, Syracuse, 1893), pp. 86-87; John Sullivan, *Journal of the Military Ex-
pedition of John Sullivan Against the 6 Nations of Indians in 1779,* (ed. Frederick
Cook, Auburn, 1887), 1-58.

10. In 1886, there were 32 extant journals of Sullivan's Expedition. The journals
are listed and described in Andrew McFarland Davis', "A Letter from Andrew
McFarland Davis to Justin Winsor" published in *1779: Sullivan's Expedition
Against the Indians of New York* (Cambridge, 1886), 3-8.

11. General John Sullivan to John Jay, September 30, 1778, cited in Otis G.
Hammons ed., *Letters and Papers of Major-General John Sullivan* (3 Vols., Con-
cord, N.H., 1939), III, 123-137.

commissioners had agreed to allow the Indians to reside upon approximately six million acres of land between Seneca Lake and Fort Niagara and to retain the right of selling it, if they desired, under the sovereignty of the United States.[12]

In the same year, however, the State of New York and Commonwealth of Massachusetts had advanced their claims to incorporate the Genesee Country within their jurisdictions on the basis of their old colonial charters. In May 1784, Massachusetts had presented a petition to Congress claiming that the charters of 1620 and 1629 had granted it all lands in the Genesee Country.[13] Congress had served notice on New York that Massachusetts petitioned for a settlement of the claim and ordered both states to present legal briefs before the Congressional commission.[14] Although New York's claim, based upon a royal charter of 1664, the submission and sessions of the Indians, and the active assertion of control by New York's colonial legislature of previous Dutch trading rights, was superior to that of Massachusetts, the controversy was not easily settled.[15]

After two year's delay, both states requested their legislatures to allow them to settle the matter outside the jurisdiction of Congress.[16] Permission was granted and agents for the states met at Hartford for a final settlement. After three weeks of negotiations, they executed a compromise agreement by which New York retained "the government, sovereignty, and jurisdiction" of all territory claimed by her; and Massachusetts obtained the right of purchasing or pre-empting all Seneca land between Seneca Lake and Lake

---

12. Barbara Graymont, *The Iroquois in The American Revolution* (Syracuse, 1972), pp. 262, 276-277, 282; George H. Harris, "The Life of Horatio Jones," Buffalo Historical Society, *Publications*, VI (Buffalo, 1903), 468-469. Hereafter cited as *BHSP*.

13. Howard L. Osgood, *"The Title of the Phelps and Gorham Purchase,"* PRHS, I (Rochester, 1892), 32.

14. *Ibid.*

15. James Duane, "State of the Evidence and Argument in Support of the Territorial Rights and Jurisdiction of New York," *Collections of the New York Historical Society* (New York, 1870), III, 122-144.

16. Osgood, *loc. cit.*, 32-33.

Erie.[17] She was also given the pre-emption right to 230,000 acres of land lying between the Owego and Chenango Rivers.[18]

Massachusetts' pre-emption right carried several important conditions which affected the settlement and development of the Genesee. First, the lands ceded to Massachusetts were exempt from federal or state taxes for 15 years from the date the Massachusetts General Court approved a purchase made by qualified negotiators.[19] Second, Massachusetts was allowed to sell the pre-emption right to whomever it deemed worthy. The only stipulation attached to a sale was that the purchaser had to have a state appointed superintendent witness the transaction, and the state had to confirm, by legislative vote, any treaty approved by the superintendent.[20] Freedom from taxation enhanced the potential value of the land, while the opportunity of purchasing part or all of the pre-emption right opened the way for private development.

Massachusetts' persistence in the matter of her charter claim may well have been based upon specific information about the region supplied to influential citizens and to members of the General Court. Nathaniel Gorham certainly knew about the commercial value of the Genesee at least as early as 1785. Gorham, who had an illustrious political career in the state and national government both as a representative and as an appointed official, became concerned with the idea of retaining the land for Massachusettes when he was a delegate to the Congress of the Confederation in 1785-86.[21]

---

17. *Ibid.*
18. *Ibid.*, 33-34; "Seed of Cession from New York to Massachusetts," Box 59, Phelps and Gorham Papers, New York State Library, Albany, New York. Hereafter cited as PGPA.
19. Osgood, *loc. cit.*, 33.
20. *Ibid.*, 33.
21. Clinton Rossiter, 1787, *The Grand Convention* (New York, 1966), 72; Peter Thacker and Thomas Welsh, *Sermon on the Dead and . . . Eulogy to the Memory of the Honorable Nathaniel Gorham, Esq.* (Boston, 1796), 5, 8, 9-14. Gorham discusses New York's plan to sell land in disputed areas west and south of the Mohawk River while Speaker of the Senate in the Congress of Confederation. See also, *Public Papers of George Clinton* (10 Vols., New York, 1899-1914), VIII, 269.

Gorham feared New York's selling the lands to speculators before a compromise could be reached.[22] At one point he supported the notion that it would be best for his state if a handsome sum of money could be obtained from New York in lieu of the pre-emption right, because controlling a remote region such as the Genesee was impossible.[23] By the end of 1786, however, the two states had solved their problems and Gorham focused his attention on obtaining the pre-emption right for his own use.

With the ownership of the Genesee Country clarified by the Hartford Convention of 1786, it remained for the General Court of Massachusetts to decide who would pioneer the Genesee. Since the General Court had the right of bestowing the pre-emption right on any person of its choosing, the process could work in a democratic manner. But, equality of economic opportunity played no significant part in the granting of the pre-emption right. The General Court's policy of viewing land as a commodity and of emphasizing the need to generate revenue was an important factor in its award. Those people who might need the land most would not be likely to be the first ones to own it.

Since the 1720's, access to new lands in Massachusetts tended to be restricted to men with capital. A need for a new land and one's ability to settle upon it were no longer basic requirements for land grants. By an act of 1727, need and settlement requirements were replaced by a bidding system whereby proprietors bought land from the colony on the basis of their ability to pay, rather than on actual need.[24] This change sharply curtailed opportunity for men of moderate means to participate directly in the initial ownership of

22. Nathaniel Gorham to Caleb Davis, February 23, 1786, Caleb Davis Papers (Boston, Massachusetts Historical Society), XIIIA.
23. Nathaniel Gorham to Caleb Davis, June 16, 1786, *ibid.*
24. Ray Allen Billington, "Origin of the Land Speculator as a Frontier Type," *loc. cit.*

wilderness territory.[25]

Massachusetts land policy also had a direct effect upon the pattern of development occurring on her new lands. Under the proprietary system, grantees became the agents for the establishment of new towns. Although proprietors did not have to settle where they purchased, they were legally responsible for surveying the lands into townships and attracting settlers to the purchase, Thus, before a pre-emption right was granted, the General Court had to be satisfied with the ability of the purchaser to perform an adequate job of developing the region.[26] In the case of the Genesee Country, one had to demonstrate a willingness to commercialize the pioneering operation, since the General Court expected to retire old Revolutionary War debts with the revenue generated by the sale of the pre-emption right.[27]

The overall effect of the Massachusetts system on the development of the Genesee Country was to encourage proprietors to promise a rational, commercially oriented development that would guarantee a rapid return on their investment and, at the same time, guarantee to the Commonwealth sufficient revenue. Thus, the General Court encouraged pioneering techniques that emphasized commercial enterprise and keen business entrepreneurship rather than piecemeal settlement by small farmers, backwoodsmen, trappers, and adventurous young drovers.

25. Ray H. Akagi, *The Town Proprietors of the New England Colonies* (Philadelphia, 1924), 10-13, 25; Melville Egleston, *The Law System of the New England Colonies* (New York, 1880), 5; Herbert L. Osgood. *The American Colonies in the Seventeenth Century* (3 Vols.; New York, 1904), I, 150-151; Charles Francis Adams, *et.al, The Genesis of the Massachusetts Town* (Cambridge, 1892), 8-10; Anne Bush Maclean, "Early New England Towns," Vol. 80, *Columbia University Dissertations* (1907-08), 20-21, 81; Florence M. Woodard *The Town Proprietors in Vermont* (New York, 1936), 14, 19, 42, 57, 61; William Haller, *The Puritan Frontier, Town Planning in New England, 1630-1660* (New York, 1951).

26. Woodard, *op. cit.,* 57, 61, 64, 74-75, 80.

27. Charles S. Grant, *Democracy in this Frontier Town of Kent* (New York, 1961), 5.

Notwithstanding the existence of orderly procedures for purchasing the pre-emption right and the legal agreeement between Massachusetts and New York concerning the disposition of the Genesee Country, wealthy and influential bidders quickly discovered that the Genesee lands were not easily obtainable. There were sufficient numbers of influential men competing for a share of the territory so that no one person or group of people could claim a firm hold on the right. Yet, in the middle of the jousting for position stood Nathaniel Gorham and Oliver Phelps.

Gorham had made a decision to attempt a purchase of the right very soon after Massachusetts completed its bargain with New York State. At first he favored making a small purchase, but after meeting with Oliver Phelps he was convinced that both men might succeed if they formed a partnership. Phelps was as convinced as Gorham that the Genesee Country was a potentially valuable piece of commercial property.

Oliver Phelps was, like Gorham, a self-made man. A precocious financial manipulator, he was 39 years old and a well-established businessman when he formed a partnership with Nathaniel Gorham. Phelps learned about the potential of the Genesee from several sources. The Rev. Samuel Kirkland, who had accompanied General Sullivan on his expedition through the Genesee in 1779, was a close friend whom he frequently had as his houseguest. Phelps' role as superintendent of beef supply for the Continental Army brought him into regular contact with cattle drovers and cattle suppliers who did a business with the British at Fort Niagara and Oswego before and perhaps during the War.[28]

There are also pieces of evidence linking Phelps to the Genesee region after the American Revolution. Phelps received an anonymous letter from a person who explored the Genesee about 1784 and who stated that Sullivan had nearly

---

28. "Phelps Geneology," Box 1, Fol. 2, Phelps Family Papers, Burton Historical Collection, Detroit Public Library, Detroit, Michigan; "Phelps Ledger Book, May 30, 1774," Box 80, Fol. 1, PGPA. Army supply accounts, 1779-1782, "Box 87, Fol. 2, 3, *ibid.*

destroyed all the old Indian settlements, leaving many tracts
of cleared lands, both upland and flatland, that were ready
for settlement and a number of good streams and good mill
sites available for development. This writer also indicated to
Phelps that he was persuaded that the Genesee would support a large number of industrious people who could make
the area blossom with agriculture and manufacturing.[29]

Phelps also learned a considerable amount of detailed information from Hezekiah Chapman, a 41 year old Yale
educated minister turned lawyer who explored the region
during the summer and fall of 1787. Chapman explained to
Phelps that a purchase of land from the Seneca Indians was
possible under certain conditions, and that a purchase was a
wise step since the Genesee was a very valuable territory.
Chapman suggested to Phelps that they form a partnership
and bid on the right. Phelps agreed with Chapman's position, provided him with shares in his newly formed land
company, but continued to seek out a partnership with
Nathaniel Gorham.[30]

When the bidding began, in 1787, Phelps and Gorham
agreed on a strategy for purchasing the right to the entire six
million acre tract and formed the Phelps-Gorham Company.
Phelps quickly put together a list of 13 wealthy and politically well-connected men who expressed interest in the enterprise. They, together with Phelps and Gorham, went forward
with a bid on the right.[31] After many adjustments and many
frustrating delays, the company successfully purchased the

---

29. "Early Descriptions of the Genesee Country," n.d., Box W-2, Hubbell
Papers, Princeton University, Princeton, New Jersey.

30. F.W. Chapman, *The Chapman Family* (Hartford, 1854), p. 197; Hezekiah
Chapman to Oliver Phelps, July 11, 1792, Box 19, PGPA; Deposition of Oliver
Phelps, September 8, 1800, Box 1801, Phelps-Gorham Papers, Ontario County
Historical Society, Canandaigua, New York. Hereafter cited as PGPC. Hezekiah
Chapman to William Walker, January 27, 1788, Box 1, Fol. 7, William Walker
Collection, Walker-Rockwell Papers, New York Historical Society, New York.
Hereafter cited as WWC.

31. *Ibid.* Orsames Turner, *History of the Pioneer Settlement of Phelps and
Gorham Purchase* (Rochester, 1851), 107-108; Phelps to Gorham, April 5, 1788,
Box 2, Fol. 1, PGPA.

pre-emption right to six million acres of land lying west of Seneca Lake on March 31, 1788.[32] The Company offered the Commonwealth L300,000 in consolidated state notes in return for the right to purchase the land from the Indians. This offer amounted to the equivalent of purchasing the land at 5ᶜ an acre. The General Court and the company believed that a low price would enable the entrepeneurs to market their land in such a way as to make it easy for the company to pay off its debt in three annual installments and turn a handsome profit in the bargain.[33]

Having secured the right, Phelps called a meeting of the proprietors to discuss financial and legal arrangements and to draw up plans for an immediate Indian purchase. The company decided to buy as much of the six million acres as the Indians were willing to sell. It also decided to send out surveyors and explorers immediately to estimate the size and value of the land, and to mark out its borders. Phelps was given authority to determine any additional work that was required to enable the company to begin selling townships as soon as possible after the Indian purchase. For that reason, Phelps requested surveyors familiar with the laying out of townships to accompany him to the Genesee.[34]

On July 8th, 1788, two months after leaving Massachusetts and one month after arriving at Seneca Lake, Oliver Phelps succeeded in convincing the Seneca Indians to sell him two million acres of land east of the Genesee River and a twelve by twenty mile stretch of land on the west side of the Genesee for $5,000. Additionally, the chiefs received an an-

32. Turner, *op. cit.*, 110-112; "Resolves of the General Court, House of Representatives, March 31, 1788," Box 1, Fol. 3, Jeremiah Wadsworth Papers, Connecticut Historical Society, Hartford, Connecticut. Hereafter cited as JWPHG.

33. *Ibid.*, "Resolution and Act Massachusetts House of Represenatives, March 31, 1788," Box 1788, PGPC; "Grant of Massachusetts . . . to Phelps and Gorham, April 23, 1788, *ibid.*

34. Oliver-Phelps to James Sullivan, n.d., Box 2 Letter Book II, PGPA; Phelps to Wadsworth, May 8, 1788, Box 1, Fol. 6, JWPHG; Phelps to Gorham, April 22, 1788, LB II PGPA, Phelps to Gorham, April 28, 1788, *ibid.*

nuity of $500 a year for life. In return, Phelps received a clear title to 2,500,000 acres of Genesee Country property.[35] The task before him was to make the lands as productive as possible, so as to pay Massachusetts what was due her and to generate profit for his fellow investors.

After completing the purchase of the pre-emption and acquiring a clear title to the Genesee lands, the company began the work of transforming the wilderness tracts into an attractive region for settlers and investors. This work involved exploring, surveying, and evaluating the quality of the land for the purpose of formulating a comprehensive policy of development. The proprietors also concerned themselves with the problems of opening up routes from the east to their new lands, so that these would become accessible to pioneers and to land speculators.

Upon Phelp's return to New England, he wasted little time in calling a meeting of the company to affirm a general plan for surveying and settling the lands.[36] The investors gathered at Zeno Parson's Tavern in Springfield, Massachusetts, on August 20, 1788, to decide how the Genesee lands would be organized for settlement.[37] The members learned that Phelps had ordered a survey of the exact north-south direction of the eastern pre-emption line separating the Genesee from the State of New York. He had also determined the actual width of the Phelps-Gorham purchase. Since the dimensions favored surveying the land into six by six square mile townships, Phelps had ordered surveyors to begin that work.[38] Phelps directed his men to lay

35. Oliver Phelps to John Butler, September 1, 1790, Box W-2, Hubbell Papers; Oliver Phelps to Daniel Penfield, Box 2, LB II, PGPA; ''Genesee Accounts,'' Box 78, Fol. 2, *ibid.;* ''Expenses of the Genesee Purchase,'' Box 17, *ibid.'* ''Genesee Country Accounts,'' Box 78, Fol. 8, *ibid.*
36. Oliver Phelps to Israel Chapin, August 6, 1788, Box 2, LB II, *ibid.*
37. Oliver Phelps to William Bacon, August 8, 1788, *ibid.;* Minutes of Phelps-Gorham Company Meeting, August 20, 1788, Box W-2, Hubbell Papers.
38. Oliver Phelps to [Anon.] August 16, 1788, Box 2, LB II, PGPA; Oliver Phelps to Roger Noble, August 8, 1788, *ibid.;* Oliver Phelps to Col. Hugh Maxwell, August 6, 1788, *ibid.*

out three ranges of townships on the pre-emption line beginning at a point about 18 miles north of the Pennsylvania border so that land might be available for sale as quickly as possible.[39] During this survey, the surveyors were instructed to note the quantity of good land, upland, sunken land, barren plains, hills and mountains contained in each township. The surveyors were also to note approximate land prices for each type of situation. Phelps temporarily set prices at 50¢ an acre for the very best land near water transportation, 25¢ an acre for rolling upland, and the very worst land at 12¢ an acre. Phelps expected to use this information when the company set the final prices during the Springfield meeting.[40]

The central question concerning the sale of Genesee land focused on the method the company would use to attract settlers and investors to the territory. There is evidence that the method of creating a high density central place and developing that town as an anchor for pioneering was well understood by the proprietary. At the Springfield meeting, Phelps put forth the view that larger profits would be realized from the sale of Genesee lands if proper measures, such as town planning and town development, were taken to foster frontier settlement. Phelps estimated that between 50,000 and 250,000 dollars profit was very likely after one year's work, and even higher profits were possible if this method was used.

In order to realize high profits, settlement had to be encouraged and an efficient means of stimulating settlement was the creation of what Phelps refers to as "city-towns" at strategic locations on the purchase. Planned towns or "city-towns" were townships containing lots of from one to ten acres each, arranged in a definite village or urban pattern designed to create a population density. The plots would contain roads and public squares and would be located at about 20 mile intervals on main water routes and roads

---

39. *Ibid.;* Phelps to Wadsworth, August 4, 1788, Box 9, Fol. 1, *ibid.*
40. Phelps to Maxwell, August 6, 1788, *ibid.*

leading from the purchase to eastern markets. The fostering of a concentration of settlers promoted higher land values and increased trade between the rural land and these commercial centers. The centers would then command the trade of their region and the import and export trade as well, thereby stimulating both commercial and agricultural development.[41]

Phelps recommended that townships that were centrally located in relation to the expected patterns of settlement and possessed high quality soil and natural transportation routes be surveyed into cities by the company. To stimulate the trading pattern between the city and the hinterland, the company would construct roads and make necessary waterway improvements to enable a profitable shipment of goods to take place on the frontier and between it and the settled regions of the east. As commercial centers surrounded by agricultural producers, cities would provide for trade and transhipment of produce back and forth between the east and the west, thereby stimulating rapid settlement and development of outlying frontier regions.

Phelps determined, that excellent sites for urban plots existed at Geneva, on Seneca Lake, at Canandaigua, at the foot of Canandaigua Lake, and at Big Tree, on the Genesee River. Since early surveys indicated that Geneva was outside the eastern pre-emption boundary, Phelps decided that Canandaigua best fit his requirement for a centrally located site. Canandaigua could serve as the county seat for the new county of Ontario, as well as service the entire region.[42]

Phelps proposed that because of the great value of city-

41. Phelps to [Anon.], August 4, 1788, Box 9, Fol. 1, *ibid.;* Phelps to [Anon.], August 16, 1788, *ibid.;* Phelps to Penfield, August 11, 1788, Box 2, LB II, *ibid.;* Orders to William Walker, agent for the Gorham, Phelps Company, August 21, 1788, Box 1, Fo. 2, WWC; Oliver Phelps to Caleb Benton, August 29, 1788, Box 2, LB II, PGPA.

42. Phelps to Maxwell, August 6, 1788, Box 2, LB II, *ibid.;* Phelps to Benton, August 6, 1788, *ibid.;* Orders to William Walker, August 21, 1788, Box 1, Fol. 2, WWC; Phelps to Benton, August 29, 1788, Box 2, LB II, PGPA; Phelps to Maxwell, August 29, 1788, *ibid.*

towns, they would remain in the possession of the company. Canandaigua, for example, would be surveyed into 120 lots, equal to the number of shares in the company, and the members would draw lots to determine how these plots were to be distributed. Under Phelp's plan, the members would be able to sell off their lands at increasing prices as settlement in the city-towns raised the value of the land in the surrounding countryside.[43]

The proprietors approved Phelp's plan to build roads on the frontier and to develop the land through series of city-towns. But they wanted to open the land in the spring of 1789, and therefore voted to survey only Canandaigua, and to open only enough roads to enable settlers to have access to Canandaigua and the Genesee River area. Because Canandaigua would serve as the administrative center of the entire purchase as well as its primary commercial market, all road and waterway work was designed to begin at Canandaigua and extend eastward toward Geneva and westward toward the Genesee River.[44]

The proprietors also settled on a policy of pricing and selling their lands to speculators and settlers. One of the proprietors, William Walker, was elected to serve as the company land agent. He was empowered to sell land only by the township. The surveying of townships into farm lots or into any other design was the responsibility of the purchaser. Settlers who could not afford to purchase a township had either to buy land from the company at a city-town or purchase lots from the owners of other townships. Thus, the company was not responsible for the detailed survey of the Genesee country, but only for the promoting of profitable land sales by merchandising their townships in a wholesale fashion. To insure profitability, the company priced their best land at $1.00 per acre, ordinary land and farmland at 50¢, an acre

43. Orders to William Walker, August 21, 1788, Box 2, Fol. 1, WWC.
44. Minutes of Phelps-Gorham Company Meeting, August 20, 1788, Box W-2; Hubbell Papers; Orders to William Walker, August 21, 1788, Box 1, Fol. 2, WWC.

and the very worst land at 16ᶜ an acre. By September, 1788, the Genesee Country frontier was thus sized up and priced by capitalists well before actual land sales and settlement took place.[45]

During the fall of 1788, the work of surveying the purchase and the plotting out of the city of Canandaigua went ahead as planned. While a party of men worked at the Canandaigua site, other workmen opened roads from Canandaigua to the Genesee and from Canandaigua to Geneva. These roads were really widened Indian paths, but they seemed sufficient to permit a horse and wagon to pass. They served to direct the initial flow of migrants toward the company's city-town and its surrounding countryside. They also served as access routes for supplies.[46]

While the so-called roads were bad, water transportation from New England to the Genesee was worse. Small boats could travel easily from Schenectady to Fort Stanwix on the Mohawk River, but beyond the fort the creeks and rivers were clogged with debris. The Canandaigua outlet, in particular, was impassable and surveyors discovered falls near the site of the proposed city that required the construction of a bypass road.[47]

While there were problems with the roads and the water routes, the company's surveying of Canandaigua went forward without any problems. By mid-November of 1788, Walker had selected a site for the city and laid out an urban plot. He had also cleared out the Canandaigua outlet and built a road around the falls. Walker selected a site on top of excellent soil on a pleasant slope about one mile from the Canandaigua Lake as the center for his new city. There he surveyed a public square for the location of county buildings. Walker then surveyed 120 one acre lots in a straight northeast

45. *Ibid.*; Phelps to Walker, September 2, 1788, Box 2, Fol. 1, PGPA.
46. Walker to Phelps, October 5, 1788, Box 1, Fol. 1, WWC; Walker, "Memorandum Book," *ibid.*; Benton to Walker, November 4, 1788, Box 1, Fol. 2, *ibid.*
47. Walker to Phelps, October 5, 1788, Box 1, Fol. 1, *ibid.*

direction from the edge of the lake, and then divided the land behind the city lots into 120 twenty acre back lots. He accomplished this task in such a way as to preserve a direct and unobstructed view of the lake for future residents. He built a small log hut to house supplies for workmen who were surveying nearby and to provide a residence for the land agent.[48] When Walker returned to New England near the end of November, the broad outline of the future civilization was in place.

During the winter of 1788-89, Phelps and Gorham spent much time on the problem of providing adequate roads and water linkage to the Genesee Country. First, the company contracted to improve the Indian paths between Fort Stanwix and Cayuga Lake and from there westward to Geneva, a total distance of about 100 miles.[49] The necessary permission required from the New York State legislature to build this road was not granted until July of 1789 when the proprietors received word that they could proceed with their project if they were willing to pay for the work themselves.[50]

While roads were slowly opened up, work on the surveying of the entire Genesee Country moved ahead nearly on schedule. By April 1789, ranges of townships six miles square, extending from Seneca Lake to the Genesee River, were surveyed and placed on maps that formally identified the location of Indian villages and important bodies of water. Phelps secured an act of the New York legislature to create the county of Ontario, which embraced the entirety of the Phelps-Gorham Purchase, and also created a county seat at Canandaigua. Thus, at the beginning of the spring migration in 1789, a county town was in place and primitive roads and open waterways were available for first comers. Although

---

48. *Ibid.;* Agreement between John McKinsty and Gorham, Phelps and Company, November 18, 1788, Box W-2, Hubbell Papers; Survey, Village of Canandaigua, 1788, Box 2, Fol. 1, WWC; William Walker, "Memorandum Book," *ibid.;* Memorandum of Agreement, October 28, 1788, Box 1, Fol. 3, *ibid.*

49. Contract, February 7, 1789, Box W-2, Hubbell Papers.

50. Gorham to Phelps, July 29, 1789, Box 17, PGPA; Gorham to Phelps, August 15, 1789, Box 17, *ibid.*

much more surveying, road building and institutional planning lay ahead, the basic design upon which this frontier was
to grow had been set in place by the members of the Phelps-
Gorham Company.

The company's agressive policy regarding the surveying of
townships and the opening up of waterways was due in large
measure to their optimistic view of the future for land sales.
Phelps argued persuasively that town planning, town
building and transportation development would generate
enough frontier development so that by the end of 1789 rising land values would yield the company great profit.[51] The
source of Phelps's optimism was what appeared to him to be
a ready market for new lands, which he believed existed in
New England, and the readiness of about one-third of the
Genesee Country to handle immediate settlement. Because
the Indians had cleared large tracts of land in the Canandaigua and Genesee River areas and in other spots on the
northern half of the purchase, Phelps predicted that at least
two thousand and perhaps three thousand settlers would take
up residence in the county during the first year of
settlement.[52]

Phelp's enthusiasm was shared by many company investors
and outside speculators who, noting public interest and
wishing to gain an early advantage, eagerly requested land
from the company. These men planned to purchase their
townships at wholesale prices and either resell them or retail
the land to settlers.[53]

Strong interest in the land was demonstrated by the
number of townships sold by the company by the end of

51. Phelps expected profits of between $50,000 and $100,000 from settling in the
Genesee. See Phelps to Wadsworth, August 4, 1788, Box 9, Fol. 1, PGPA.
52. Phelps to Wadsworth, May 8, 1788, Box 1, Fol. 6, JWPHG; Phelps to
Wadsworth, April 5, 1788, ibid.
53. Phelps to Benton, August 29, 1788, Box 2, LB II, ibid.; Bacon to Walker,
August 30, 1788, ibid.; Josiah Burr to Jeremiah Wadsworth, March 10, 1788, Box
1, Fol. 6, JWPHG; Burr to Wadsworth, May 12, 1788, ibid.; Walker, "Memorandum Book," Box 1, Fol. 1, WWC.

1788. Out of 45 townships surveyed, the Phelps-Gorham Company had sold thirty. Although this number represented two-thirds of the total available for sale, these sales were far below Phelps' original estimate of fifty.[54] Furthermore, out of thirty townships sold, sixteen were purchased by members of the land company. Since the cost of an average township was about 4,000 dollars, and since the proprietors purchased them mainly on credit, the company failed to realize much revenue from these sales.[55] Yet it had to generate a quick return on its investment to meet its financial obligation to the Commonwealth of Massachusetts, as well as to meet its own target for profit.

During the winter of 1788-89, Phelps and Gorham set certain policies that they hoped would stimulate Canandaigua settlement. Phelps increased the size of the city lots from one to ten acres in order to satisfy prospective settlers who complained that they did not wish to settle on such small lots. Next Phelps priced his city lots at one dollar per acre and farm lots at 50ᶜ an acre. These prices were well below equivalent lands in New England which retailed for ten to twenty dollars an acre in 1789.[56] Besides offering the buyer attractive pricing, Phelps held out the promise of company support for the construction of a handsome new community in a relatively short period of time. Phelps established a plan that required city land owners to erect decent dwelling

54. Phelps to [Anon.], n.d., Box 2, Fol. 1, Box 2, LB II, PGPA; Phelps-Gorham Company Meeting, January 13, 1789, Box W-2, Hubbell Papers; Phelps to Sullivan, April 14, 1788, Box 2, LB II, PGPA; Phelps to Wadsworth, June 6, 1788, Box 2, Fol. 1, *ibid.*

55. List of Conveyances to Robert Morris, n.d., Box 78, Fol. 8, PGPA; Land Sales in the Genesee, 1788, Box 2, Fol. 7, *ibid.;* Minutes of the Phelps-Gorham Company Meeting, January 13, 1789, Box W-2, Hubbell Papers.

56. "Sale of Land in Townships 10, Range 3," Box 70, Fol. 2, *ibid.;* "Sales of Lots in Townships 10, Range 3," Vol. 130, LR, *ibid.;* Harry J. Carman, ed., *American Husbandry* (New York, 1939), 68; Kenneth Lockridge, "Land, Population and the Evolution of New England Society, 1630-1790," in *Colonial America* (ed. Stanley N. Katz, Boston, 1971), 473-476; Davis M. Ellis, *Landlords and Farmers* (Ithaca, 1946), 25-26.

houses on their lots within a short time after settling in order
to stimulate the creation of a residential community. The
company also planned to support the construction of public
buildings, such as a courthouse and jail on the village green,
as soon as it was practical to do so in order to promote Canandaigua's function as the county seat.[57] Most importantly,
Oliver Phelps and other proprietors indicated that they were
going to build houses and establish businesses in Canandaigua in order to stimulate its function as the territorial
center of commerce.

Of all the company policies designed to create a focus for
pioneer settlement, the decision by Phelps and others to actually become pioneers in the Genesee Country had the far-
thest reaching consequence for the development of that territory. During the spring of 1789, twelve proprietors, including Phelps, built residences in the city and formed the
nucleus of Canandaigua's pioneer settlement.[58] Their purpose in settlement was to pursue their private interests as well
as to oversee company business related to town development.
But their impact upon the town was significant. By the end
of 1789, these men established regular commercial contact
between Canandaigua and the New England and Albany
areas. With the supplies shipped from the east the proprietors quickly erected stores and grist and saw mills, and
established land businesses for the convenience of settlers.[59]
By the summer of 1789, the town had an adequate supply of
groceries, building materials, hardware, and dry goods.
Taverns and inns were erected and sturdy log buildings were
built to house pioneer businesses. By combining land
business with retail sales and services, these proprietors effec-
tively organized the frontier trading pattern around Canan-

---

57. Memorandum of Agreement, November 22, 1788, Box 1, Fol. 3, WWC.
58. Augustus Porter, "Narrative of Early Years," BHSP, VII (1904), 279-280.
59. Samuel Beckwith to Oliver Phelps, February 5, 1789, Box 1789, PGPC;
Oliver Phelps to Esq. White, February 4, 1789, Box 2, LB III, PGPA.

daigua, making it the principal focus of frontier commerce throughout the entire purchase.[60]

Settlement of the proprietors not only made Canandaigua the center of land sales and trade, but also the principal financial center, where every important economic transaction occurred. The opening of the Genesee Country attracted the presence of a variety of people. There were 36 men employed by the company to survey and to work on roads. There were also land speculators, settlers, Indian traders, itinerant peddlers, Indians, and various opportunists flocking to look at the Genesee lands.[61] Since money and supplies and labor were scarce, proprietors and other men of capital became the frontier's first bankers. These men were the source of credit settlers required to purchase supplies. They cosigned loans, endorsed IOU's, and helped put into local circulation currency needed for everyday business transactions. Businessmen also stablized the barter system by setting up markets for trade in land, labor, and supplies.[62] The localizing and regularizing of financial operations enabled many pioneers to pay what they owed to the company.

Non-proprietary, business-oriented settlers supplemented the efforts of the company members in establishing Canandaigua as a commercial center. Although many of these pioneers were not wealthy, they made significant contributions to settlement.[63] Eight men accounted for the establishing of three general stores, two taverns, two hotels, and a tannery.[64] Aside from creating additional trade activi-

60. Receipt for hollow ware, January 14, 1789, Box 1, Fol. 4, WWC; Shipping bill, June 4-August 1789, Box 78, Fol. 8, PGPA; Oliver Phelps in account with Apollos Hitchcock, August 18, 1789, Box 87, Fol. 1, *ibid.*

61. See numerous receipts, accounts and notes referring to work records of Phelps and Gorham personnel in Box 87, Fols. 1-8, and Box 87, Fol. 1, PGPA.

62. Oliver Phelps to John Van Eps., July 2, 1789, Box 2, Fol. 1, *ibid.*; Walker, "Memorandum Book," Box 2, Fol. 1, WWC

63. *Ibid.*; Oliver Phelps to Elisha Talmadge, June 26, 1789, Box 69, Fol. 4, PGPA.

64. W.H. McIntosh, *History of Ontario County, N.Y.* (Philadelphia, 1876), 11.

ty, these establishments eased the shortage of space available for eating, sleeping, and doing business.

Thus, within one year of settlement, the activities of pioneering investors had succeeded in transforming Canandaigua from a vacant wilderness area into a frontier boom town filled with residents, surveyors, explorers, traders, and laborers. Houses were built, taverns and inns were in place. Indeed, Canandaigua after a year of settlement was a growing and busy place.[65] With this consideration in mind, Oliver Phelps planned additional measures to enhance Canandaigua's position as the commercial center of the Genesee Country and its image as a place of power and prosperity.

Accordingly, Phelps encouraged the replacing of rudimentary log cabins serving as stores and dwelling places with larger, more elegant frame buildings.[66] Although construction was difficult due to spot shortages of materials, he and his fellow investors erected frame houses, barns and stores as quickly as they were able. By 1792, the outline of what was to become Canandaigua's first generation of handsome architecture was dwarfing the rough-hewn structures of the first settlers. These new, substantial and attractively built houses lent grace and dignity to the small town, and conveyed to visitors a feeling of growth and prosperity.

Phelps was also prepared to erect a courthouse and jail on the village square and put a first-class hotel near the center of town. He believed that a functioning legal system and a comfortable inn would attract lawyers and merchants and give the town a good reputation among influential travellers. He also reserved lots of land for the establishment of a minister and for a school, in order to promote the town as "respectable."[67]

65. Turner, *op. cit.*, 163-164.
66. Memorandum of Agreement, Walker and Chapin, November 23, 1788, Box 70, Fol. 2, PGPA.
67. Gorham to Phelps, July 22, 1788, Box 17, *ibid.*; Gorham to Phelps, August 15, 1788, *ibid.*; Phelps to Gorham, August 28, 1789, Box 2, Fol. 1, *ibid.*

As a result of town building policies and local land promotion, Canandaigua property sold well. During the first full year of settlement, 39 men purchased 42 lots in the commercial center. In the township, twenty-one farm lots were sold, mostly to speculators, reflecting the notion that as the village grew, the outlying region would become more valuable. As in the sale of townships, sales in the center and on the perimeter were made in large measure to company proprietors who felt strongly that the Genesee Country held a great future.[68]

Actual settlement during the first year in Canandaigua was encouraging. Sixteen settlers took up residence in the township, including five people on farm lots and eleven in the city. The city population contained a mixture of business interests, but the principal business was merchandising. For example, four men engaged in retailing dry goods, three were primarily interested in land sales, two ran taverns and inns, one provided blacksmithing and leather dressing service and one engaged in farming. Thus, ten of sixteen settlers, or 62% of the residents of the village, were commercial rather than agricultural in their orientation.[69] The settlement and early development of Canandaigua had some effect upon the sale and settlement of other townships in the purchase. By the end of 1789, the company had sold 46 townships, more than ⅔ of these located within 12 to 18 miles of Canandaigua. Virtually every township near Canandaigua had been sold. Although these towns were purchased on the merits of their good soil as well as their proximity to a planned town, there is no doubt that the presence of a commercial center

68. "Sale of Lands in Township 10, Range 3," Box 70, Fol. 2, *ibid.* See also numerous landsales in various townships in "Maps, Surveys and Conveyances," Vol. 139a, LR, *ibid.*

69. The pattern of settlement can be determined from land sales lists. See "Sale of Lands" in T 10, R 3, Box 70, Fol. 2, *ibid.*

and the availability of road and waterways enhanced their attractiveness to the purchasers.[70]

The success of the Phelps-Gorham Company in selling most of its townships was not reflected in the amount of money collected from the sales. Most of the townships were sold on credit and many of them were sold to members of the proprietary so that the company could expect little cash until the investors were able to retail their land to settlers. Another reason for the company's precarious financial situation was the fact that Phelps and Gorham expected to pay their debts with near worthless state securities which, in late 1789, started to rise in value as public expectation over the possibility of the federal government redeeming state debts became apparent. In fact, these securities rose from 37^c on the pound to $1.25 by the time Phelps' and Gorham's first payment was due to the Commonwealth. Securities became scarce as well as expensive as 1790 approached.[71]

The company's basic problem was a lack of cash. Phelps calculated that no more than one third of the sales made in the Genesee would produce cash before their debt of L30,000 to the Commonwealth came due.[72] After the company expended considerable efforts to avoid a lawsuit over this matter, the General Court brought suit against the company in January, 1790.[73] The company, in turn, sought and was granted a continuance of the case for six months so it might

70. Phelps to Gorham, July 14, 1789, Box 2, Fol. 1, *ibid.;* "Land Sales in the Genesee," Box 2, Fol. 1, *ibid.;* Turner, *op cit.,* 142; Phelps to Noah Phelps, January 29, 1789, Box 2, LB III, *ibid.*

71. Joseph S. Davis, *Essays in the Earlier History of American Corporations* (2 Vols.; Cambridge, 1917), I, 187-188; E. James Ferguson, *The Power of the Purse* (Chapel Hill, 1961), 195-196; Phelps to Samuel Street, February 14, 1789, Box 2, LB III, PGPA; Phelps to Gorham, November 9, 1788, *ibid.;* Phelps to John Williams, January 28, 1789, *ibid.*

72. Phelps to Street, October 6, 1788, Box 2, Fol. 1, *ibid.*

73. Phelps to Walker, December 9, 1789, Box 1, Fol. 5, WWC; "Writs of Suit Against the Land Holders of the Phelps-Gorham Company," November 25, 1789, *ibid.*

negotiate a compromise solution with the General Court.[74]

After six weeks of discussion with members of the state legislature, a solution was worked out and the company formally petitioned the General Court for relief.[75] The company requested the Commonwealth to assume ownership of the right to purchase all their land west of the Genesee River, and allow the company to develop one quarter, or approximately one million acres, of this land as agents of the state. In return, the state agreed to release the company from paying the last two bonds due, and relinquished one year's interest on the bond they held. The company agreed to pay off the final one third due on the first note. The petition was accepted by the assembly on March 1, 1790, and on March 5, Governor John Hancock signed the bill which ended the dispute.[76]

Several weeks after completing this agreement, Phelps and Gorham received an offer from Robert Morris to purchase all remaining company lands east of the Genesee and to share in their agreement with Massachusetts west of the river. After lengthy negotiations, the proprietors and Morris signed an agreement transferring all unsold lands, including lands that remain unsold along the northern border of the Phelps-Gorham purchase, to Robert Morris for L35,000.[77] This transaction actually generated sufficient income to enable the members of the Phelps-Gorham Company to realize a profit on their initial investment. The company books showed that the proprietors had debts of L54,666 and credits totalling

74. Phelps to Walker, December 9, 1789, *ibid.*; Gorham to Theodore Sedgwick, January 27, 1790, Vol. A, Fol. 5, Theodore Sedgwick Papers, Massachusetts Historical Society, Boston, Massachusetts. hereafter cited as TSPM.

75. Gorham to Sedgwick, January 27, 1790, Vol. A, TSPM; Gorham to Sedgwick, January 30, 1790, *ibid.*

76. "Petition of Phelps and Gorham to the Massachusetts General Court," February 26, 1790, Box W-2, Hubbell Papers; "Proposal of Phelps and Gorham to the Massachusetts General Court," n.d., Box 78, Fol. 8, PGPA.

77. Penfield to Phelps, August 16, 1790, Box 17, *ibid.*; Simeon DeWitt to Oliver Phelps and Nathaniel Gorham, Jr., August 10, 1790, Box 17, *ibid.*; Gorham to Phelps, November 21, 1792, Box 19, *ibid.*

L52,420 as of June, 1790. The sale to Morris and income produced from miscellaneous sales boosted company income to
L96,722 by the end of 1790. As a result, Phelps was able to
offer his investors a dividend of L253 for each share of stock
they held in the company. He was able to do this on the basis
of the company's net profit of L42,126.[78]
     Although the Phelps-Gorham Company passed out of ex-
istence in 1791, it left behind a sturdy foundation on which a
new frontier civilization could develop. Between 1791 and
1800, Oliver Phelps and other proprietors who established
residence in Canandaigua continued to influence its development as a central place on the frontier. Phelps went ahead
with his plan to help establish churches and schools in the
village and a judicial system for the entire county of Ontario.
The judicial framework, consisting of Justices of the Peace,
courts of the General Session of the Peace and a court of
Common Pleas, was created by law in January, 1789 at the request of Phelps.[79] This law stipulated that a jail be constructed and that a sheriff, marshall, and county clerk be appointed by the New York Council of Appointments. Phelps
sent the Council a list of men he deemed eligible for these
positions and they were duly appointed. These men were
company shareholders, large landlords, and generally well-
educated and well-connected friends of Phelps'. Thus the
core of Ontario County's frontier leaders were mainly eastern
gentry transplanted to the Genesee Country.[80]

---

78. See account of the profit, 1791, Box 2, Fol. 3., *ibid.;* Oliver Phelps to Elisha
Lee, April 22, 1791, Box 78, Fol. 3, *ibid.;* "Gorham, Phelps and Company in ac-
count with Oliver Phelps," April 1, 1790-March, 1791, Box 78, Fol. 2, *ibid.*
     79. Oliver Phelps, "Petition to the New York Legislature," February 7, 1792,
Box 3, Fol. 1, *ibid.;* Oliver Phelps, "Memorial to the New York State
Legislature," December 31, 1788, PGPC; *Laws of the State of New York,* III,
12th Sess., Chap. 11, pp. 10-11.
     80. Jedidiah Morse, *The American Geography* (2d ed.; London, 1792), 272;
Gorham to Phelps, July 31, 1789, Box 17, PGPA; Phelps to Gorham, July 14,
1789, Box 2, Fol. 1, *ibid.;* Phelps to Thompson, April 10, 1790, Box 2, Fol. 1,
ibid.; Phelps to Gorham, March 31, 1790, Box 2, Fol. 1, *ibid.*

The building to house the judiciary was also a project that engaged Phelp's attention. Since state and local taxes could not be collected for public construction because of the Hartford agreement, Phelps petitioned the New York legislature for a special law enabling a tax to support the building of a courthouse.[81] Permission was granted and work immediately began on a courthouse and jail. Phelps loaned $200 to the project in lieu of taxes and collected loans from other citizens so that a two story log house was raised by the end of 1792.[82] An excellent two story frame courthouse, with an attractive spire was completed at the end of 1794. In addition to money, Phelps contributed glass, paint, nails, and milling services to the project, and when completed, the courthouse stood as a significant achievement among his many frontier enterprises.[83]

Establishing educational and religious institutions was an important part of Phelp's plan of city development. He wanted Canandaigua society to reflect values which he considered important in older, settled communities. By making Canandaigua a center for frontier education, Phelps promoted the development of his city and the region.[84] Phelps encouraged qualified men to settle in Canandaigua and teach in its school. He did this by offering to pay their teaching salaries and by granting generous terms on town lots. Phelps contributed money towards the building of small log cabins that served as elementary schools, so that by 1792 the center of Canandaigua possessed a decent primary school staffed by qualified teachers.[85] In addition to this, Phelps

---

81. Oliver Phelps to the New York State Legislature, February 7, 1792, Box 3, Fol. 1, *ibid.*
82. Phelps to n.n., February 20, 1792, VII, Western Mementos, New York Historical Society, New York; Judah Colt to Oliver Phelps, September 18, 1792, Box 19, PGPA.
83. Oliver Phelps to Israel Chapin, August 9, 1794, X, Western Mementos, New York Historical Society, New York.
84. Annual Oration, Canandaigua Academy, n.d., PGPC.
85. John Taylor to Phelps, January 27, 1792, Box 19, PGPA; Canandaigua School Committee to Oliver Phelps, March 24, 1792, *ibid.;* Jared Root to Oliver Phelps, November 28, 1796, Box 23, *ibid.*

established an academy of higher learning for young men
and women in the town. In 1789, he and Gorham set aside
six thousand acres of land and created a board of trustees to
administer the assets of an academy. In 1795, when population in Canandaigua and surrounding townships reached a
sufficient level, Phelps secured a charter from the state
legislature to start the Canandaigua Seminary. School was
held in the courthouse until 1797 when a modest frame
building was near the village center on land donated by
Phelps.[86]

Religious institutions played an equally important part in
the shaping of community values and in Phelps' plan for
developing a frontier community. The need for establishing
churches, in particular, was evident to Phelps during the first
year of settlement, but neither Phelps nor Gorham was able
to attract a permanent minister to Ontario County until
1796, and not to Canandaigua until 1799.[87] Dangers and
hardships associated with frontier living, including the
presence of malaria, dissuaded ministers from heeding
Phelps' call. Part time ministers such as Zadock Hunn, a
Congregationalist from Becket, Massachusetts, rode a circuit
in 1796, attending to the needs of frontier settlers.[88] But it
was not until 1799 that Canandaigua established two
churches, a Congregational and an Episcopal one to serve the
needs of 100 families in the town.[89] Phelps aided the Congregational Society by providing money and land for the sup-

86. Phelps to Gorham, August 28, 1789, Box 2, Fol. 1, *ibid.;* Phelps to Chapin,
August 15, 1794, X, Western Mementos, NYHS; Oliver Phelps To Dudley
Saltonstall, February 17, 1797, Box 4, Fol. 1, PGPA; Annual Oration, Canan-
daigua Academy, n.d., PGPC.

87. James H. Hotchkin; *History of the Purchase and Settlement of Western New
York* (New York, 1848), 24-26.

88. *A History of the County of Berkshire, Massachusetts* (Pittsfield, 1829), 308;
James Wadsworth to Oliver Phelps, April 2, 1792, PGPA.

89. Nathan Barton to Oliver Phelps, August 9, 1791, *ibid.;* Phelps to Chapin,
August 16, 1792, Box 2, Fol. 1, *ibid.;* James Wadsworth to Oliver Phelps, April 2,
1792, *ibid.*

port of the minister, and substantially aided in the recruitment of the Rev. David Field of Yale College, who took the
call as the first full time pastor of the Congregational
Church.[90]

Phelps' significant accomplishments in establishing
churches, schools, and a county judiciary system were aided
by the completion of a road network leading from the
Genesee Country to the east. The process by which Canandaigua grew from a collection of log huts and cabins to a busy
commercial and agricultural center by 1800 was directly
related to changes in population, rates of agricultural production and the rise of efficient transportation between the
frontier and the settled east. Phelps was a moving force
behind this phase of development and his efforts contributed
directly to the growth in economic prosperity and social
development experienced in Canandaigua between 1790 and
1800.

Frontier roadbuilding, commenced in 1788 by the Phelps-
Gorham Company, was designed only to link the Genesee
Country with the Mohawk River. By 1791, about 60 miles of
road were opened up through eight thinly populated
townships stretching between Avon and Canandaigua. By
1795, 167 miles of new road linked settlers in every direction
with Canandaigua. By 1800, Canandaigua commanded the
trade of a wide region through a network of 251 miles of in-
terlocking roads and waterways.[91]

Roads connecting the west with the east, however, were
mostly inadequate for frontier needs. The Phelps-Gorham
proprietors knew that their original road system was only the

90. Notice of the First Congregational Church at Canandaigua, February 25,
1799, Box 2, Vol. A, Ontario County Court Records, Canandaigua. Hereafter
cited as OCCRC; Trustees of the First Congregational Society of Canandaigua to
Oliver Phelps, December 4, 1799, Box 29, PGPA; McIntosh, *op. cit.*, 34; Notice
of the Episcopal Church at Canandaigua, February 4, 1799, Box 2, Vol. A, OC-
CRC.
91. Augustus Porter, "A Map of Gorham and Phelps Purchase," Phelps-
Gorham Book of Maps, Hubbell Papers.

first step toward establishing reliable communication with the east. By the end of the decade, the New York legislature agreed with Phelps that a better road was required.[92] In 1800, an act to allow for the establishment of a turnpike road company for building a toll road from Utica to Canandaigua was passed.[93] The so-called Seneca Turnpike Company was formed to construct the road. This company was an amalgamation of frontier capitalists, like Phelps, who expected to profit by its activities.[94] The road was built in three sections with Phelps sponsoring the road between Geneva and Canandaigua.[95] The system was completed in 1803 and opened for business in 1804 at a cost of $1,000 per mile.[96]

There were many defects in the road system, but the turnpike did lower the cost of transporation to the Genesee country.[97] Instead of paying $16.00 per ton for goods shipped by water, merchants could ship goods by road from Utica for $1.83 per ton.[98] Since more goods could now be carried faster, greater efficiency, lower prices, and higher profits for merchants resulted.

The result of Phelp's effort in creating a city in the wilderness is rather startling. In 1789, only William Walker's solitary log cabin existed at Canandaigua. By 1794, the village possessed a wide main street, sloping gently upward for two miles from the lake and touching a public square in the center of town. From this vantage point, one could clearly see the result of Phelp's policy. Forty houses lined the edge of Main Street, all framed, attractively painted, and many

92. George S. Conover, comp., "Canadasaga and Geneva" (unpublished manuscript in Buffalo Historical Society, 1886), pp. 119-120.
93. *Ibid.*, 122.
94. Dudley Walsh to Oliver Phelps, July 6, 1797, Box 25, PGPA; Chapin to Phelps, June 14, 1800, Box 30, *ibid.*
95. *Ibid.*
96. Canandaigua turnpike contract, February 19, 1802, Box 93, Fol. 1, *ibid.*; Receipt for funds, February 26, 1802, *ibid.*
97. N.n., to Prince, January 16, 1805, Box 6, *ibid.*
98. Conover, comp., *loc, cit.*, pp.122-126; McIntosh, *op. cit.*, 28, 30, 54-55.

surrounded by neat gardens and lawns.[99] By 1800, the village contained over 70 homes and possessed a handsome church with steeple rising in the middle of town overlooking the lake.[100]

The growth of business in Canandaigua paralleled its residential growth. The town started with approximately fifteen businesses in 1790 but by the early 1800's, this number grew to 45.[101] In 1818, a survey of local businesses listed 36 stores, 36 shops, 30 offices, 14 taverns, and 153 stables.[102] In terms of business development, the town had grown substantially from a thinly settled outpost offering only a limited amount of growth, to an economically diversified regional center.

The role played by Oliver Phelps and his fellow proprietors cannot be underestimated when one considers the pioneering experience of central New York. As the pioneering agency, these individuals, working together and later separately, planned and executed the organization and development of both the township of Canandaigua and nearly half of the entire Genesee Country. By practicing a deliberate policy of urban settlement, they avoided haphazard settlement and slow development. By treating land as a commodity, these business people promoted a rapid rise in land values and in trade. Thus, the city of Canandaigua, centrally located on good soil and possessing water and road communication with eastern markets was the essential instrument used by men of capital in pioneering the Genesee Country. The configuration of the city was an important element in establishing merchants and farmers as frontier settlers. In this context,

99. Duke De La Rochefoucault Liancourt, *Travels in North America* (2 Vols.; London, 1799), I, 146.

100. Timothy Dwight, *Travels in New England and New York* (New Haven, 1822), IV, 30-31; Francis Hall, *Travels in Canada and in the United States in 1816 and 1817* (London, 1818), 115.

101. Jedidiah Morse, *American Gazetteer* (Boston, 1797), 74-75.

102. Business census. See William Darby, *A Tour from the City of New York to Detroit* (New York, 1819), 133-134.

Phelps worked diligently at promoting social and economic institutions that fostered the rise of new civilization. In the hands of Oliver Phelps, town planning and frontier development became effective tools for pioneering the New York frontier.

NEW YORK AND ITS NEIGHBORS:

SOME PROBLEMS OF

REGIONAL INTERPRETATION

D. W. MEINIG

The place of New York in the history and character of American development has been a chronic problem for interpretation. As you all know, the relative neglect of New York and/or the "Middle Colonies" and their successor states has been a recurrent topic in American historiography for forty years. Eric Goldman's brief review of 1941 on interpretations of the role of the "Inbetweeners" defined some aspects of the issue: neglect was measured by the small proportion of attention given to those colonies lying between Connecticut and Virginia, to the section between New England and the South; whether this was the result of regional bias on the part of particular influential historians or because any incipient Middle States regionalism became transmuted into American nationalism he left uncertain.[1]

Two years later Richard Shryock, with his special concern for Philadelphia, speculated on the theme at greater length and argued for the need to foster a strong civic and Middle Atlantic regional tradition comparable to those of New England and the South. Twenty years later he was still complaining of this neglect, although he now used it as an argu-

---

1. Eric F. Goldman, "Middle States Regionalism and American Historigraphy: A Suggestion", in Eric F. Goldman, ed. *Historiography and Urbanization. Essays in American History in Honor of W. Stull Holt* (Baltimore, 1941; reissued Port Washington, N.Y., 1968), 211-220.

ment against an overemphasis on regionalism.[2] Meanwhile
Brinton Thompson was offering what was evidently the only
college course on the Middle Atlantic region (and doing so in
the midst of Yankeedom at Trinity College, Hartford), and
in 1956 he presented his ideas in a rather shrill book whose
title *Gateway to a Nation* could be taken in both an historical
and geographical sense.[3] David Ellis, from his deep-rooted
Upstate perspective, applauded Thompson's intent and offered his own succinct complaint over the neglect of New
York and the Middle Atlantic region.[4] More recently, Milton
Klein has published a series of essays on the theme, arguing
for the specific importance of New York[5], and Michael Kammen pointed out how "incredible" it was that his 1975 book
in the History of the American Colonies series was the first
"biography of early New York" to appear since 1919.[6]

---

2. Richard H. Shryock, "Historical Traditions in Philadelphia and in the Middle
Atlantic Area: An Editorial", *The Pennsylvania Magazine of History and
Biography*, 67 (1943) 115-141, and "The Middle Atlantic Area in American
History", *Proceedings of the American Philosophical Society*, 108 (April 1964)
147-155. His fellow Pennsylvanian, Frederick B. Tolles, thought that "the Middle
Colonies can hardly be called a region," but agreed about their neglect, noting
that "most historians" end by characterizing them in terms of some vague "mid-
dleness" derivative from the two vividly different regions on either side; Tolles,
"The Historians of the Middle Colonies," in Ray Allen Billington, editor, *The
Reinterpretation of Early American History, Essays in Honor of John Edwin Pomfret* (San Marino, CA, 1966), 65-79.
3. The reference to his course is in Ellis, note 4, below; D.G. Brinton Thompson
"The Middle Atlantic States and Their Influence on the Development of the Nation", in George I. Oeste, editor "New Viewpoints in the Teaching of Social
Studies", *Annual Proceedings of the Middle States Council for the Social Studies,
1949-50*, v. 47 (Philadelphia, 1951); D. G. Brinton Thompson, *Gateway to a Nation*, (Rindge, N.H., 1956).
4. David Maldwyn Ellis, "New York and Middle Atlantic Regionalism", *New
York History*, 35 (1954) 3-13.
5. See especially Milton M. Klein, "New York in the American Colonies: A New
Look", *New York History* 53 (1972), 132-156 and reprinted in Klein, *The Politics
of Diversity, Essays in the History of Colonial New York* (Port Washington, N.Y.,
1974), and "Shaping the American Tradition: The Microcosm of Colonial New
York", *New York History* 59 (1978) 173-197.
6. Michael Kammen, *Colonial New York, A History* (New York, 1975).

By 1979 Daniel Greenberg could open his review of recent
writings on the Middle Colonies by noting that this relative
neglect of the area had "become something of a cliché"
among historians. He went on to make clear that these recurrent statements were more than a plea for "equal time,"
they were in the main an argument about relative
significance, an insistence that contrary to the massive
literature and indoctrination about Puritans and Cavaliers,
the Middle Colonies, and in some ways especially New York,
more clearly "pre-figured" the character of the nation; that
here more than in New England or Virginia was the
"microcosm," the "embryo," the "paradigm of what
America at large would become" (these last three terms are
characterizations by Klein, Bonomi, and Kammen, respectively).[7]
As all of these writers were aware, this view of the primary
significance of the region as "typical" had been set forth un-
compromisingly long ago:

The Middle region, entered by New York harbor,
was an open door to all Europe.. [and] was less
English than the other sections. It had a wide mixture of nationalities, a varied society, the mixed
town and county system of local government, a
varied economic life, many religious sects...It
represented that composite nationality which the
contemporary United States exhibits,...It was
democratic and nonsectional, if not national;
"easy, tolerant, and contented"; rooted strongly in
material prosperity. It was typical of the modern
United States.[8]

7. Douglas Greenberg, "The Middle Colonies in Recent American
Historography", *The William and Mary Quarterly*, 3rd series, v. 36 (1979)
396-427. On the three terms cf. Klein, note 5 above, Patricia U. Bonomi, "The
Middle Colonies: Embryo of the New Political Order", in Alden T. Vaughan and
George Athan Billias, *Perspectives on Early American History, Essays in Honor of
Richard B. Morris* (New York, 1973), and Kammen, *op. cit.*, xvi.

Now that poses a puzzle: how can we speak of neglect in the face of such a statement of 1893 in the body of the most influential interpretation ever set forth in American historiography? Pursuit of a solution to that would lead us astray from my main purpose, however an important factor is latent in those phrases of Frederick Jackson Turner: they indicate a variety, a heterogeneity, a complexity that is difficult to analyze and assess, an ensemble of features which provides no unifying theme, no obvious clear focus for a penetrating interpretation. As Greenberg notes, there has been marked progress in the characerization of New York political life (especially by Bonomi, Klein, and Kammen), and illumination of community and larger social history, but still no general regional interpretation comparable to those available for New England and Virginia. In general university textbooks this Middle Region remains rather in a shadow in colonial history. At best its importance may be asserted but not demonstrated. Typically in national history, earlier regionalism is broadened into the sectionalism of North, South, and West, but with little indication of just how a North takes shape from earlier patterns. Thus, New York remains a problem in American historiography.

To say that New York is also a problem in geographic interpretation would, I fear, be forcing the parallel a bit. American geographers have never given much attention to internal political areas, have rarely defined their problems in terms of states, but rather have devised their own sets of regions to serve particular purposes. However, it is apparent that the general area of the Middle Atlantic states has been a problem in certain kinds of geographic interpretation. Our concern is less a search for parallels than for hints at possibilities for convergence upon some common topics.

---

8. Frederick Jackson Turner, ''The Significance of the Frontier in American History'', Amerian Historical Association, *Annual Report for 1893* (Washington, 1894), 220.

In America, the field of geography was grounded in physiography and long remained closely associated professionally with geology. When geographers moved to make greater connection with broad human topics it was logical that they would begin with what seemed to be the fundamental influences of the gross structure and character of the land. In the New York area that great glacial spillway, the Hudson-Mohawk Depression, forming a unique breach through the Appalachian Highlands, was a feature of great human as well as natural prominence. Two books published in 1903 which became fixtures on the reading list for generations of history classes, Albert P. Brigham's *Geographic Influences in American History* and Ellen C. Semple's *American History and its Geographic Conditions,* agreed that the quality of New York harbor and its great natural corridor inland, together with relative location on the continent and with respect to Europe, made New York the true ''keystone'' of the seaboard states and New York City inevitably the dominant center.[9] This kind of simple inferential ''logic of the land'' (including climate as well as terrain) became deeply embedded in American history and social science as ''the geographic factor,'' one of the several basic ''factors'' that must be taken into account in the study of human affairs. But it was always regarded as the simplest, a ''given'' that seemed to require little analysis. As such, geography was routinely treated as a basic setting, a stage for the human drama which set certain conditions and limits; in historical writings geography was a preface, a groundplan set forth before the action begins, to be kept in mind as the plot unfolds but with no significant effect upon the detailed character of the drama itself. This view of geography became dominant in American academic and public life sixty or more years ago and, alas, remains not uncommon today.

---

9. Albert P. Brigham, *Geographic Influences in American History* (Boston, 1903), esp. 4-26, 32; Ellen Churchill Semple, *American History and Its Geographic Conditions* (Boston and New York, 1903), esp. 17-18.

As the field of geography further enlarged its attention upon man, it did so not by focusing directly upon the human drama and joining with history to study processes and events in the actual development of areas, but by applying its energies to the detailed study of the current character and use of areas, creating a special and rather limited form of human ecology. In such studies history became no more than a preface to geography, a background sketch of a few main events leading to present patterns.

J. Russell Smith, the most eloquent and influential interpreter of the geography of North America for many years following the publication of his great textbook in 1925, divided the continent into more than forty "human-use regions." New York State was bisected by the urban-industrial corridor of the Erie Canal Belt, "one of the most clear-cut regions in North America" laid down by nature between the Northeastern Highlands and the Appalachian Plateau. (Figure 1) The Coastal Plain, Northern Piedmont,

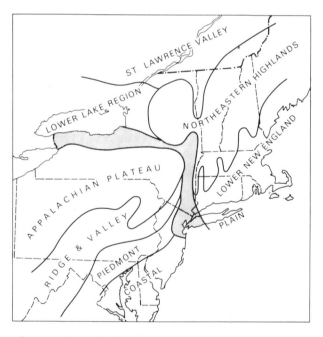

Fig. 1. The Erie Canal Belt and other "human-use regions," as defined by J. Russell Smith, 1925.

Appalachian Ridge and Valley regions cover the rest of the area of the Middle Atlantic states.[10] Smith provided a detailed and lively description of each of these regions, noting current socio-economic problems and offering his opinions as to the wisdom or folly of policies relating to land and resources. His book is basically an economic geography of physical regions. The logic of the land is still powerful.

Smith's treatment of New York implicitly displays the problem of reconciling a regionalization system closely reflective of the physical qualities of the land with human-use patterns which are more directly part of secondary and tertiary economic networks. After all, Binghamton, Corning, and Elmira, deep in the Northern Appalachians, were as fully urban-industrial in economic base as many of the cities of the Erie Canal Belt. One solution which became long common in geography textbooks was a partial separation of economic sectors in order to recognize a broad "Manufacturing Belt" extending from the northeastern seaboard to Chicago-St. Louis, studded with urban-industrial centers and interacting through a complex network of transportation facilities, all superimposed upon a great diversity of physical-agricultural regions.[11] Such regionalization was a step toward recognition of a major imbalance in a national structure which was something more than a sum of discrete physical-human use parts. It hinted at the concept of a core area which exercised major influence upon the operation of a national system.

Such a view becomes much more explicit in John Paterson's *North America,* a book widely used for the past twenty years on both sides of the Atlantic. Having discussed

10. J. Russell Smith, *North America, Its People and the Resources, Development, and Prospects of the Continent as an Agricultural, Industrial, and Commercial Area* (New York, 1925), 125. For a good example of a similar basic regionalization adapted to historical periods see Raymond E. Murphy and Marion Murphy, *Pennsylvania, A Regional Geography* (Harrisburg, Pa., 1937, figures 18, 22, 25).

11. Probably the most widely used text with this treatment was C. Langton White and Edwin J. Foscue, *Regional Geography of Anglo-America* (New York, 1943 and several subsequent editions).

some inherent problems of regionalization as a descriptive and analytic device, he begins his survey with the Middle Atlantic Region (approximately the states between the Hudson Valley and the Potomac) because:

> whether judged by its share of population, industry, or foreign trade of the continent, or by its wide control of the nation's business, this region's primacy is abundantly evident.

And having described basic patterns of economic activities, he goes on to stress the complex direct power of the region in national life:

> Industry and transport and enterprise elsewhere in the United States are directed from this core, which is a kind of general headquarters of Enterprise America, the national economy, even when the actual production processes are carried on in other regions. This region makes decisions not only as to when and on what terms finance shall be provided, but equally what the nation shall read (for it dominates the publishing business), and how American goods shall be advertised or presented...Not milk nor steel nor chemicals, but decisions are the chief output of the Middle Atlantic region.[12]

Unfortunately these remain a set of assertions rather than an introduction to an analysis of how the nation functions as a spatial system in these terms. The fault is not Paterson's but of a field which has yet to provide a sufficient monographic literature devoted to such topics.[13]

---

12. J.H. Paterson, *North America, A Geographic of Canada and the United States,* (Sixth edition, New York, 1979), 174, 182.

13. A beginning was made by Edward L. Ullman in "Regional Development and the Geography of Concentration", *Papers and Proceedings of the Regional Science Assocation,* 4 (1958) 180-198, and there is of course an enormous literature bearing upon the topic, but no really coherent geographical analysis. The capacious survey by Harvey S. Perloff, *et.al, Regions, Resources, and Economic Growth* (Baltimore, 1960), offered an economic history perspective, using states and groups of states as data units.

It should be clear from all this that regions are abstractions. They are geography's analogy with history's periods: created by human minds as a means of imposing order and making sense out of an infinitude of data. This was strikingly illustrated by the sudden appearance in 1961 of a new region which quickly altered common perceptions of our geography and added a new name to our vocabulary: "Megalopolis," that almost continuous system of deeply interwoven urban and suburban areas stretching along the northeastern seaboard from northern Virginia to New Hampshire. (Figure 2) Labeled "the Main Street of the Nation," it was described

Fig. 2. Megalopolis, as defined by Jean Gottmann, 1961.

as a region incomparable in role, unsurpassed in importance, supreme in politics, economics, and cultural activities.[14]

14. Jean Gottmann, *Megalopolis, The Urbanized Northeastern Seaboard of the United States* (Cambridge, MA, 1961).

Megalopolis was presented to the public by Jean Gottmann, a French geographer deeply conscious of history and human agency. Thus while focusing most of his attention on the contemporary scene (in keeping with his commission from the Twentieth Century Fund), he draws upon history throughout to offer some sense of development and continuities, and he insists that the character, scale, and momentum of this geographic phenomenon cannot possibly be understood without taking into account "the spirit of the people", which he believes has been expressive of a blend of Turner's frontier and Perry Miller's errand into the wilderness unleashed and shaped within the flexible framework of the *Novus Ordo Seclorum* of the Republic.

Megalopolis has had a major impact upon the way we perceive the geography of the United States[15] (although looking over this 20-year old book today one cannot but be struck with how dated it has become, given the sudden and massive shifts in population, economic development, and political climate of the past few years). I am not aware that it has had any impact at all upon how we perceive the history of the United States, although the general outline of a major historical development together with some tentative explanations and interpretations are laced through the book. As a geographic interpretation it states forcefully that this massive metropolitan concatenation has submerged older regional distinctions along the seaboard and has differentiated this coastal strip from the hinterlands of its constituent cities. In the case of New York, Megalopolis underscores the primacy of downstate-upstate regionalization in contrast to an Erie Canal Belt or a Middle Atlantic region.

Two final items in this introductory reconnaissance will add further complications but also suggest more explicit con-

---

15. e.g. Stephen S. Birdsall and John W. Florin, *Regional Landscapes of the United States and Canada* (New York, 1978), and the lates edition of C. Langdon White, Edwin J. Foscue, and Tom L. McKnight, *Regional Geography of Anglo-America* (Englewood Cliffs, N.J., 1979).

nections between the perspectives of geography and history. They come from the subfield of cultural geography and are thereby grounded upon rather different evidence marshalled for different purposes than that of the economic geography which has dominated the American field. Wilbur Zelinsky's small 1973 book, the first interpretative synopsis of the cultural geography of the United States, was an entirely fresh work larded with provocative ideas. Among these is his annotated map of culture regions with its several levels of differentiation.[16] New England, the Midland, and the South are delimited as first-order regions. (Figure 3) Within the

Fig. 3. Two levels of "major traditional culture Areas," adapted from Zelinsky, 1973.

Midland he draws a second-order cultural boundary between the Pennsylvanian Region and the New York Region along a line generally parallel with but approximately a tier of coun-

16. Wilbur Zelinsky, *The Cultural Geography of the United States* (Englewood Cliffs, N.J., 1973), 118-9.

ties south of the state line, a delineation supported by
evidence from studies of "language, religion, house types,
and town morphology," which together reflect different
streams of early migration within these two sub-regions.
Zelinsky's alternative name for the New York subregion,
"New England Extended," defines a major characterizing
impact of that migration. Yet, as he notes, the evidence is
not clear-cut and it "presents the cultural geographer with a
major classificatory dilemma":

> Perhaps it is sensible to think of it as a hybrid place
> formed mainly from two parental strains of almost
> equal potency: New England and the post-1660
> British element moving up the Hudson Valley and
> beyond. In addition there has seen a persistent, if
> slight residue of early Dutch culture and some sub-
> tle filtering northward of Pennsylvanian influences.
> Evidently, it is within the New York subregion that
> we find the first major *intra*-American blending
> and fusion of regional cultures, most particularly
> within the early nineteenth-century Burned-Over
> District in and near the Finger lakes and Genesee
> area. This locality, another of the many about
> which we still know much to little, is notable in two
> respects. It was the seed bed for a number of im-
> portant innovations; and it was also a major staging
> area for westward migration and quite possible the
> chief source for the people and notions that were to
> build the Middle Western Region.[17]

General recognition of a strong New England immigration
and influence upon Upstate New York is of course commonplace among historians. Turner describes this at some
length, and *The Expansion of New England* by his student
Lois Kimball Mathews has been a standard reference on the

---

17. *Ibid.*, 127.

topic since 1909.[18] Nevertheless, Zelinsky's comments and kinds of evidence point to much work to be done to refine our understanding.

In his 1975 book *Cultural Regions of the United States* Raymond Gastil acknowledged a heavy debt to Zelinsky even though he set forth a different set of regions. He put particular emphasis on Zelinsky's "Doctrine of First Effective Settlement" which states that

> the specific characteristics of the first group able to effect a viable, self-perpetuating society are of crucial significance for the later social and cultural geography of the area, no matter how tiny the initial band of settlers may have been.[19]

Gastil considered that the Yankee imprint upon New York has been sufficiently indelible to warrant putting the whole of the Upstate area into a greater "New England Culture Region," differentiating it by primary boundaries from Metropolitan New York and from a Pennsylvania Region. (Figure 4) However, he, too, saw this apportionment as a difficult problem in geographic interpretation which "is open to a great deal of question" and "awaits better regional analysis."[20] Gastil, who is by training a cultural anthropologist, also drew upon a diverse and rather eclectic array of recent social and cultural indicators, including data on religion, political culture, voting patterns, dialect, education, rates of homicide, and infant mortality in determining his regions.

---

18. F.J. Turner, "Greater New England in the Middle of the Nineteenth Century", *American Antiquarian Society Proceedings*, n.s. 29 (1919) 222-41, *The Nation and its Sections*, esp. the maps p. 97 and "Interstate Migration, 1850" in the appendix, n.p; Lois Kimball Mathews (Rosenberry), *The Expansion of New England: The Spread of New England Settlement and Institutions to the Mississippi River, 1620-1865* (Boston, 1909).

19. Zelinsky, *op. cit.*, 13; Raymond D. Gastil, *Cultural Regions of the United States* (Seattle and London, 1975), 27.

20. Gastil, *op. cit.*, 152,153.

Fig. 4. "Culture Regions and Districts," adapted from Gastil, 1975.

It may be pertinent to remark at this point that while all these maps might be thought of as "games geographers play" (and there is a long history within the field deriding regional geographers as those who "put boundaries that do not exist around areas that do not matter"[21]), or merely a set of pedagogic compartments for the packaging of facts for undergraduates, they at least imply important ideas about the structure and character of the United States. They are partial interpretations of how New York fits within that national structure and of how it is related to other regions. They contain assertions as to how such patterns came to be and what they signify. Regionalism is itself a theory and a method and has at times been translated into a philosophy and a movement. It should be noted that the civic and personal values of fostering a greater regional self-consciousness are asserted in those early essays of Richard Shryock and David

---

21. H.T. Kimble, "The Inadequacy of the Regional Concept", in L. Dudley Stamp and S.W. Wooldridge, editors, *London Essays in Geography* (Cambridge, 1951), 152-173.

Ellis, and they are the central theme of Raymond Gastil's book. Gastil's hopes of using regionalism as a means of reshaping public policies and combating "the crisis of meaning in our lives" recalls the Odum school of regional sociology and the fears of Leviathan prominent in the 1920's and 30s.[22] However we may feel about the virtues, limitations, or dangers of this theory, method, and movement, regionalism is something more than playing around with maps.

Even so brief a reconnaissance suggests how disparate in focus, methods, vocabulary, and purpose the literatures of history and geography have been over many decades. Nevertheless, it is possible to identify some topics of at least implicit convergence wherein we might describe some bases for collaboration in our studies of New York. I shall suggest two rather general topics and comment on some possibilities for research. These are, first, relationships between New York and New England, and, second, relationships between New York, the Middle Colonies and successor states, and the development of a national core area. Were there time to do so, I should like to have commented on New York and its neighbor to the north, for I believe that the signficance of that border zone and the separateness of the literature of the two countries cries out for greater attention to New York-Canadian relationships over the full span of our histories.

There are two general propositions about New York and New England that are confirmed in virtually all our literature. One is that they began and remained throughout the colonial period, and for some uncertain time after, as two distinct regional cultures. Underneath any generalizations we might make about European colonizations and frontier pro-

---

22. Gastil, *op. cit.*, "Conclusion", 289-306. Howard W. Odum and Harry Estill Moore, *American Regionalism: A Cultural-Historical Approach to National Integration* (New York, 1938); Donald Davidson, *The Attack on Leviathan: Regionalism and Nationalism in the United States* (Chapel Hill, N.C., 1938).

cesses the differences in people, their historical experiences, and the societies they created are sufficiently clear as a general feature as to need no elaboration here. Nor is this a matter of modern scholarly definition only. The most telling fact is the historical evidence that each of these regional peoples saw themselves as different from the other, and indeed not only different, but wherever in close contact likely to be in some degree antagonistic to one another. Dixon Ryan Fox's classic *Yankees and Yorkers* remains the most apt characterization of these two and their relationships.[23] The criteria for such characterizations may be debatable without challenging the basic integrity of the two societies.

The second proposition about New York and New England is that when western New York was opened for settlement in the first decade of the republic New Englanders migrated and settled in such numbers upon so wide an extent of country during this community-forming period as to stamp an indelible Yankee imprint upon the subsequent history and character of all Upstate beyond the Hudson and Middle Mohawk valleys. This general feature is also widely accepted, although interpretation in detail remains uncertain at best. Probably the most prominent and influential presentation has been Whitney R. Cross, *The Burned-Over District, The Social and Intellectual History of Enthusiastic Religion in Western New York, 1800-1850.*[24]

These two propositions are of course interlocked; they are sequential and interdependent, the regional characteristics defined by the first giving point to the process and imprint created by the second. Together they impinge directly upon most of the regionalizations we have reviewed.

The most basic historical geography research topic relating to the first proposition is definition of the location and character of the boundary between these two regional

---

23. Dixon Ryan Fox, *Yankees and Yorkers* (New York, 1940).
24. Ithaca, N.Y., 1950.

cultures. Some years ago I offered a simple approximation of this divide as it was on the eve of the Revolution, based upon a reading of town histories.[25] (Figure 5) But we need a more

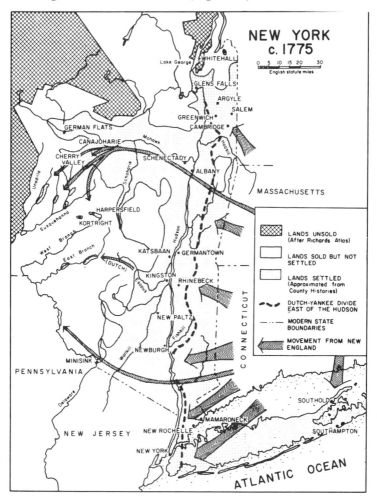

Fig. 5. *Approximation of the boundary between New York and New England regional cultures, c. 1775. Reproduced from Thompson,* Geography of New York State, *by permission of Syracuse University Press.*

25. Fig. 41, 'New York c 1775'', in John H. Thompson, editor, *Geography of New York State* (Syracuse, 1966), 133.

detailed depiction of the complexities of the spatial relationships between these two peoples at various times. We need to
examine it at the scale of localities to try to see it in terms of
the social geography of daily life. We may expect to find that
in any particular era this may vary from no contact at all, the
two peoples being separated by several miles of wasteland, to
a common border wherein the farms of Yorkers and Yankees
directly abut on one another, to a shared zone wherein the
two peoples are intermingled, to a serration of long salients
where Yorkers had early moved eastward up the valleys and
Yankees later spread westward along the higher ground between, to enclaves of Yankee farmers dominating localities in
the midst of generally Yorker districts, to Yankee development of Hudson River ports and drawing in the trade of
whole sectors of Yorker countryside. Nor should we forget
that this cultural border zone extended to East New Jersey as
well, initiated by New Haven Puritan colonizations at
Newark, Elizabeth, and Woodbridge just beyond Dutch settlements in Bergen County, and by the more mixed New
England influx, including Baptists and Quakers as well as
Calvinists, from Long Island, Rhode Island, and
Massachusetts to Piscataway, Middletown, and Shrewsbury.[26]

I am aware that historians have paid a great deal of attention to conflicts associated with this political border zone,
and that interpretation, especially of recurrently violent
landlord-tenant disputes, has given rise to considerable controversy among historians themselves as they have tried to
sort out and assign weight to property interests, social status,
class alignments, political factions, and colonial allegiances
in these complex affairs. Without insisting upon the primacy
of the differences in regional cultures, of what may well be
called the ethnic dimension in these disputes, it does seem to

---

26. Peter O. Wacker, *Land & People, A Cultural Geography of Preindustrial
New Jersey: Origins and Settlement Patterns* (New Brunswick, N.J., 1975), 122ff.
John E. Pomfret, *The Province of East New Jersey 1609-1702* (Princeton, N.J.
1962). Thomas Jefferson Wertenbaker, *The Founding of American Civilization,
The Middle Colonies* (New York, 1938), Chapter 4.

me that the clearest possible depiction of this geography of encounter would provide great illumination. For example, the significance of that head-on collision between Yankees and Yorkers is central to most of Philip Schwarz's recent meticulous study of "New York's Boundary Makers," yet it is never directly defined on a map and therefore one can never make full sense of the political issues in each area.[27] I would venture that much of the information needed for such maps could be distilled from historical and geneological documents already familiar to specialists. The geographer's most obvious contributions could come from interpretation of such materials in the field, from reading the evidence of field patterns, architecture, road connections, and village morphologies apparent in the landscape today, and from devising cartographic means to generalize the complexities of such detailed archival and field evidence into the most reliable analytic tools.

This reference to field research is a reminder that the topic is not simply one of colonial history, it extends as far toward our own time as any significant distinction remains between these two peoples in this border zone. The history of encounter and conflict merges into the history of local societies wherein consciousness of Yankee and Yorker identities may persist in church affiliations, social clubs, political behavior, moral codes, and marriage patterns for generations. Where all such distinctions fade into insignificance there remains the problem of defining the result: acculturation? convergence? assimilation? but to what end? forming what product? As David Ellis has noted with respect to the Albany-Troy area, the antagonisms between Yankee and Yorker softened as they increasingly came to see themselves as the old responsible members of society threatened by the influx of Roman Catholic Irish.[28] But did such a common stance

---

27. Philip J. Schwarz, *The Jarring Interests, New York's Boundary Makers 1664-1776* (Albany, 1979).
28. David M. Ellis, "Yankee-Dutch Confrontation in the Albany Area", *New England Quarterly* 45 (1972) 262-270.

lead to a complete fusion and translation of old identities into a WASP Americanism, or was it an alliance between
peoples still conscious of their differences, a Yankee ingre-
dient adding further complexities to an ongoing developing
Yorker culture? Answers can only come from social histories
of communities undertaken with this kind of cultural
regionalism as an important part of the context. Here I find
myself sympathetic to Alice Kenney's recurrent pleas to pay
more attention to those traditions which shape people's
private worlds, to that subtle ethnicity that may persist un-
noticed by those who focus on major public events, issues,
and movements.[29] It is a plea for a scale and sensitivity in
social history akin to that of the keen student of the vernacular landscape;[30] bringing these together could produce
the kind of penetrating humanistic historical geography
which one can envision but not yet display.

The question of what happened when Yankees and
Yorkers encountered one another and competed for control
of local districts leads directly into our second proposition
about the broader Yankee impact upon Upstate New York.
Here the topic is certainly complex. The literature tends to be
broadly impressionistic or narrowly focused in time, place, or
topic, and prescriptions for improvement must be selective
and partial, for the ramifications range far beyond the pur-
view of any practitioner.

It is easy for my kind of historical geographer to say what
one would most like to have in hand for his study of such a
topic. It would be an atlas of migration: a set of maps showing sources, routes of movement, and places of settlement of
the migrants to this huge frontier over the first thirty or forty
years after the Revolution. There would have to be
simplifications, and one would be willing to forego detailed
data on some of the internal dynamics of this general coloni-

---

29. Alice P. Kenney, "Private Worlds in the Middle Colonies: an Introduction to
Human Tradition in American History", *New York History* 51 (1970) 4-31.
30. Cf. Stephen W. Jacobs, *Wayne County: The Aesthetic Heritage of a Rural
Area* (Lyons, N.Y., 1979).

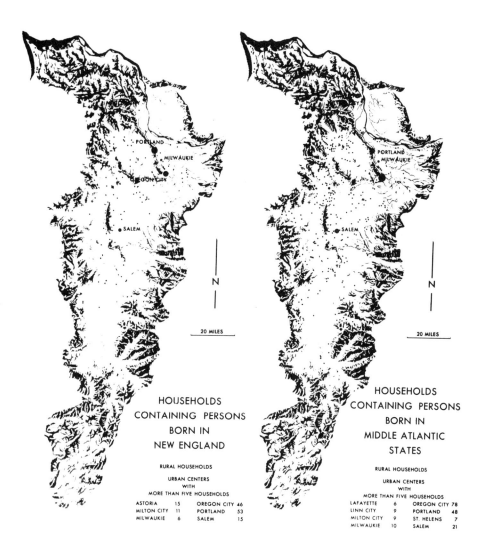

Fig. 6. Mapping, Willamette Valley population data of 1850. Reproduced from Bowen, The Willamette Valley, *by permission of the University of Washington Press.*

Fig. 7. Inferred kinship ties. Reproduced from Bowen, The Willamette
Valley, *by permission of the University of Washington Press.*

zation process, such as the instability of settlers, the selling
and re-selling of lands, if one could have a fairly good account periodically of who was actually living where, if not
house by house at least by local districts or towns. It is easy to
say that given the data available such an atlas is quite beyond
hope; but why not ask instead: "how close can we come to
creating such a set of maps?" At this point it seems fair to say
that given the range of data available: "a great deal closer
than we now are." William Bowen's remarkable study of the
Willamette Valley in Oregon in 1850 is an exciting example
of what might be accomplished.[31] (Figures 6 and 7)

The creation of such an atlas would be a formidable and
costly undertaking requiring many skilled workers, and I
speak of it not as an incipient proposal but only to insist that
progress on some basic questions requires that we work
toward a better sense of the presences and proportions of the
varieties of migrant peoples who domesticated and
developed this frontier, a clearer view of the social surface of
Upstate and adjacent areas.

We would find, of course, a good deal of unevenness in
that surface. There were certainly communities founded by
and wholly stocked with New England migrants, and there
were whole counties with large Yankee majorities. Yet in
nearly every town, certainly in every larger district and county, there were other people as well, people who had no
background connection whatever with New England and its
peculiar regional culture: people from the Hudson-Mohawk
Valley, New Jersey, Pennsylvania, Maryland; new immigrants from England, Wales, Ulster, Scotland, Holland,
France, and various parts of Germany; people in great ethnic
and religious variety. The main fact is that whatever the
numbers of Yankees who came to Upstate they had to share
this new region with others to a degree and in ways unlike

---

31. William A. Bowen, *The Willamette Valley, Migration and Settlement on the
Oregon Frontier* (Seattle and London, 1978).

anything they could have experienced in their former homes. Thus Upstate could never become a simple extension of New England nor a western replica of what had been the most homogeneous regional society in the colonies.[32]

Even if by assiduous research we could create such maps, the real problems of interpretation would remain. What are New Englanders supposed to have brought with them—a form of community, a particular polity, a special religious intensity, a set of moral attitudes, a zeal for social improvement, an unusual energy, inventiveness, restlessness? Historians have been struggling to define and measure such things for years. One of the apparent truisms, and complexities, is that not all New England groups were the same. In the older Turnerian view, the selectivity of migration and the experience of pioneering made the Upstate Yankee less conservative, less Puritan, more adaptable, more tolerant than his New England brethren; whereas historians reacting against such frontier interpretations emphasize the opposite, that the migrants were more conservative and less tolerant, for they were undertaking a new errand into the wilderness to reestablish that which had been lost in lax, materialistic, strife-ridden Massachusetts and Connecticut.[33] There is evidence for both views and one way of reconciling them is to differentiate by place, to refine our depiction of this social surface so as to distinguish between "progressive" and "conservative" communities. The practicalities of such a sorting are doubtful, however; not only are the data elusive, one suspects that a close reading of that available would expose the inadequacy of such classifications. But we might try to identify areas of group migration where some cadre of settlers attempted to

---

32. There was some religious variety in New England but mostly among people who had been an integral part of the regional society for generations, such as local dissidents, Baptists, and Quakers, or members of an indigeneous revitalized Anglicanism. The few Ulster Irish and German immigrants were mostly shunted to the northeastern fringes.

33. Page Smith, *As a City Upon a Hill, The Town in American History* (New York, 1966), is a prominent example of emphasis upon the latter interpretation.

replicate the community form of the New England town and village together with its institutions. And we can try to identify experimental communities and those villages and budding cities wherein important social innovations were attempted. The difficulty is that to do this requires a formidable amount of sensitive research at a community level, and the special geographical difficulty is the "tyranny of the map"; the geographer's abhorrence of having areas left blank because "unknown," the urge to connect the social contours on this surface, and thus the demand for comprehensive coverage.

One might well postulate that most New Englanders came hoping to better themselves whilst matter-of-factly carrying the common baggage of Yankee culture with them. Some adaptation to new circumstance was to be expected. The degree of divergence between the new region and the source region would depend in part upon the links maintained between the two. In geography jargon, focus on the continuing spatial interaction after migration would be a critical topic, and might include studies of social ties through letters, visits, marriages; intellectual ties through publications, schooling, itinerant preaching, and leadership recruitment; business ties in finance and commerce. The general question posed might be phrased: did New England *send* its culture westward, or did it *extend itself* westward? If the former, we may expect continuing divergence as the original agents of the culture (the migrants) adapt, disperse, and become steadily distanced in time from their New England roots; if the latter, we are defining a kind of geographic growth which can only be maintained by efficient channels of communication. Thus we need to know a good deal about roads and turnpikes and the kinds of traffic and messages moving along the trunklines and circulating through local communities during the first forty years of federal life.

The most obvious geographic feature in this interregional relationship is the intervening position of the Hudson Valley. All links between New England and Central New York had to traverse a well-settled longitudinal band of Yorker country, an important complication impinging upon any simple concept of "New England Extended." Furthermore, all overland traffic between the two areas had to defy the lure of the greater ease and economy of Hudson River services. Water was the great medium of bulk transport and New York City was in fact pivotal to much of the trade between New England and Upstate. We may in general suppose that the Hudson Valley and the Catskills did little to deter Yankee migration westward, but had considerable effect upon the maintenance of close social relations thereafter, and that the Hudson and the Berkshires made it impossible for Boston to compete with New York City for general Upstate commerce prior to the railroad. Nature's great channel was indeed a powerful factor in the shaping of such economic regions.

One further complication should be noted. Concepts of "New England Extended" tend to measure Upstate against an "entity" called "New England culture" defined in terms of colonial characteristics (and these are often defined more in terms of early Puritan rather than later Yankee features). But of course the early federal years are a period of great dynamic development in an industrializing and commercializing New England, as well as in the newer Western regions. Indeed the dense pattern of what came to be accepted as the typical New England village is in some ways more a product of this national era than of the colonial period.[34] Thus we need to compare New England and New York in terms of concurrent developments as well as sequential, and to assess what similarities we find as to whether they are diffusions westward from New England, or parallel features within distinct regional components of a national system.

This New England impact upon New York has been so emphasized in our literature that we may underestimate

---

34. Joseph Sutherland Wood, "The Origin of the New England Village," Ph.D. Dissertation (Geography, The Pennsylvania State University, 1978).

other sources of people and interregional connections. The Hudson Valley together with western Long Island and East New Jersey was of major importance but rather difficult to trace and assess because most of it was "intrastate" and because the character of each local area in such a heterogeneous source region is difficult to identify.

Another source and connection was Pennsylvania, together with adjacent parts of Maryland, Delaware, and West New Jersey by way of the Susquehanna. Speculators in Philadelphia and Baltimore were heavily involved in western New York lands. The geographic strategists sent to shape the development of great tracts, such as Charles Williamson and Joseph Ellicott, envisioned the Susquehanna as a great entryway, Baltimore as the natural seaport, Philadelphia as the obvious cultural, financial, intelligence, and immigration center. From their respective "capitals" at Bath and Batavia, these men constructed roads and facilities, imported supplies and machinery, organized cattle export drives, recruited settlers and employees, and in general operated primarily in terms of this Susquehanna axis for some years, as evidenced in their records and notably in the base maps they commonly used. (Figure 8) So long as such things were being managed from Philadelphia the superiority of the Mohawk route was not obvious nor would it have been demonstrable in every case.[35] Not until the War of 1812 and its sudden military demands did the Mohawk-Erie axis begin to emerge as clearly dominant. To be sure, the Susquehanna route fell short of early expectations, but we are far from having an adequate assessment of what the contributions from this direction were.

---

35. The relative significance of these Susquehanna and Philadelphia connections will be clarified by much new data and the careful assessments of William K. Wyckoff in his doctoral dissertation "Joseph Ellicott and the Western New York Frontier: Environment Assessments, Geographical Strategies, and Authored Landscapes, 1797-1811" (Geography, Syracuse University, 1982). The Adlum and Wallis map was widely used during this decade, as apparent in the Holland Land Company records in Buffalo and Amsterdam.

Fig. 8. A Geographical and Hydrological Map, Exhibiting a General View of the Roads and Inland Navigation of Pennsylvania and Part of the Adjacent States, by John Adlum and John Wallis, Philadelphia, 1791. Copy courtesy of William Wyckoff.

Influence of course is not to be measured just by numbers of settlers and volumes of commerce. If you roam leisurely through central and western New York today along the lesser roads, savoring the landscape, indulging in that pleasant game of guessing from the first glimpse of steeple or tower what breed the main village church will prove to be, your best bet is: "Methodist." Now that is an interesting fact and one that might give pause to acceptance of some common assumptions about regional relations. Methodism is no extension from New England. Quite the contrary, it was a keen competitor to Puritan and Presbyterian Calvinisms. As a for-

mal denomination the Methodist Episcopal Church was
established at Baltimore in 1784, and it grew and spread with
such astonishing vigor that by 1850 it was the largest
denomination in twenty states, including New York.[36]
Methodism came to New York out of Philadelphia, primarily
by way of the Susquehanna and the Lycoming and Tioga
valleys. It spread far more by conversion than by migration.
Its remarkable circuit rider system took religion to the frontier, brought it within reach of every settler, and it was a
system in place ready to share in the harvest of souls to be
gathered in the wake of the great revivals which repeatedly
swept through the "burned-over district." Many, perhaps
even most, of those who became Methodists in New York
were actually of New England birth or parentage, but even so
they had thereby become something other than a Yankee
transplanted. Just what they had become may be hard to
define. It was part of that first intra-American blending to
which Zelinsky referred. It was not a simple inter-regional fusion; it did not make them Penn-Yans—half Pennsylvanian,
half Yankee—for Methodism had no such distinct
geographic connotation. Coeval with the Republic, it was
broadly American in character and was more a cultural instrument of nation-building then of regional formation.[37]

If you extend your landscape explorations and roam on
southward, the state boundary seems to make little difference. New Milford and Montrose, Troy and Canton,
Mansfield and Wellsboro look much the same as nearby
towns in New York. But if you venture much farther the
change becomes unmistakable. When you get to the Lycoming and the West Branch or beyond the great coal complex of

---

36. Edwin Scott Gaustad, *Historical Atlas of Religions in America* (New York 1962), 74-82.

37. I base my remarks on Methodism upon the work of Michael J. Nickerson who is preparing a doctoral dissertation on "The Geographic Strategies of the Methodist Episcopal Church in its Expansion into the Northeast, 1785-1810" in the Geography Department, Syracuse University.

Scranton and Wilkes-Barre to the rural reaches of the Susquehanna toward Bloomsburg and Sunbury, the architecture
and building materials, farmsteads and towns, all those indelible features of the formative layers of the cultural landscape are strikingly different. If we are uncertain just what influences did come up the Susquehanna, it is quite clear that
the German barn, the "I" house, widespread building in
brick, and the general design and internal density of Pennsylvania towns did not reach much beyond Williamsport and
Wilkes-Barre. This evidence of one of "the sharpest architectural divides in North America," reinforced by the findings
of folklorists, linguists, and toponymists is basic to the
regional delimitations of Zelinsky and Gastil.[38] (Figures 9,

*Fig. 9. Upstate vernacular: the classical temple "upright and wing", still
widespread in town and countryside. Courtesy of Peirce F. Lewis.*

10, 11 and 12) They have taken it as evidence of a strong New
York-New England connection. It is certainly fundamental
to the assessment of interregional relationships and it is an
imprint that remains to be appreciated, integrated, and further examined by historians.

38. The quotation is from Peirce F. Lewis, "Common Houses, Cultural Spoor",
Landscape 19 (1975) 1-22. It is reforced by Zelinsky: "the particularity of its [Pen-
nsylvania Culture Region] town morphology is especially striking . . . the urban
centers, large and small, of New York and Pennsylvania's Northern Tier are cast
from an utterly different mold", in Wilbur Zelinsky, "The Pennsylvania Town:
An Overdue Geographical Account", *The Geographical Review* 67 (1977)
127-147; the references in this article are a good guide to the main supporting
studies, to which should be added Zelinsky's "Some Problems in the Distribution
of Generic Terms in the Place-Names of the Northeastern United States", *Annals, Association of American Geographers* 45 (1955) 319-349.

Fig. 10. Pennsylvanian vernacular, the "I" house and German forebay barn. Courtesy of Peirce F. Lewis.

This sharp landscape boundary bears directly upon con-
notations given to the Middle Colonies and the Middle
Atlantic states as a region. It attests that New York and Pennsylvania were largely distinct and separated settlement areas
during a formative period, and to put them together is more
an arbitrary grouping of contiguous areas that fit some
general type, than recognition of a regional system of interacting parts which might have created a geographic surface of
common cultural features. It is clear that historians have
recognized a middle region on the basis of some shared
general characteristics, emphasizing the heterogeneity of
peoples and the complexities of societies, politics, and
economies, which distinguish New York, New Jersey, and
Pennsylvania from New England and the Chesapeake.
Detailed analyses have been much more by state than by
region, and if, for example, New Jersey and Pennsylvania
developed "techniques of political management and party
building" similar to that of New York to cope with the tur-
bulent and competitive factionalism of the many contending
peoples, as Patricia Bonomi has argued,[39] it was apparently

---

39. Bonomi, *op. cit.* 91.

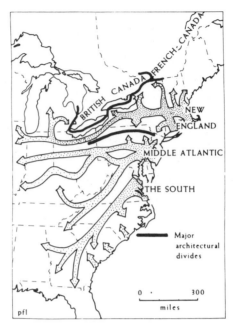

Fig. 11. "Westward migration of architectural ideas," by Lewis, drawing upon Kniffen and Glassie. Reproduced by permission from Landscape.

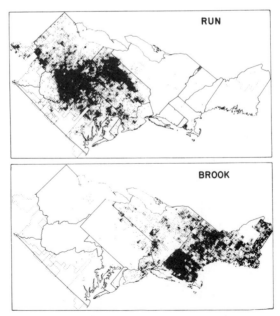

Fig. 12. Two terms illustrating toponymic regionalism, from Zelinsky; reproduced by permission from The Annals of the Association of American Geographers.

more the result of parallel response to a common kind of problem than of a direct diffusion of ideas within the three-colony grouping, although that question may be worth exploring.

The bi-polarity of the Middle Colonies, anchored upon Philadelphia and New York City and dividing New Jersey between them, is of course an indelible feature; the individuality and rivalries of the two great cities are still there within all the intricate structures and pulsations of Megalopolis. The intense historical competitions between the two and with other major seaports for both trans-Atlantic and trans-Appalachian trade have been extensively studied, the individuality of each in the development of its local hinterland and range of specializations has been recognized if less commonly stressed. In any case, emphasis upon the special character of each of the two cities and each of the states tends to undermine the concept of Middle Atlantic regionalism.[40]

But concurrent with these rivalries and distinctions there was an interaction between the two cities which was not only of regional but national importance. If we wish to examine the Middle Atlantic area as a regional system we must focus attention upon the links between New York City and Philadelphia as the obvious main axis. Indeed, the historical geography of that routeway is surely one of the major topics in the study of nation-building. Our concern must be with spatial interaction, with the movements of messages as well as of people and goods. Detailed examination of the sequence of physical facilities, from the earliest ferries and road improvements through all the eras of transport development is fundamental, to which must be added studies of the succession of services provided. Much information on all these matters is already available in topical and local studies, but it

40. Thomas C. Cochran, "The Middle Atlantic Area in the Economic History of the United States", *Proceedings of the American Philosophical Society*, 108 (1964) 156-157.

must be put into the context of the dynamics of regional and national integration.[41]

Much the most seminal work I know of is Allan R. Pred's *Urban Growth and the Circulation of Information,* published in 1973, which analyzes and graphically depicts spatial biases in the diffusion of European news, in postal services, interurban travel, and the interurban spread of innovation.[42] The early emergence of New York City as "the principal node of the nation's information system," and of the Boston-Baltimore axis as always "at least one step ahead" of other links in the speed and frequency of such circulation and in interurban interdependence is clearly defined with some interesting documentation.[43] The exciting feature of Pred's work is his elucidation of the emergence of regional and national systems of interaction. One need not be put off by his rather strident assertion of himself as a scientist interested more in theory and models than in history, and his concern "for using analyses of the past as inputs in the development of regional planning policies."[44] He is here a creative historical geographer who has pointed the way toward the kind of dynamic regional analysis necessary if we are to answer the questions implicit in the concerns of historians and geographers about the role of New York and the Middle Atlantic area. Pred's study takes us through the "pre-electronic" era, that is, up to the advent of the telegraph. We need to carry on such analyses of interaction right up to the Eastern Airlines Shuttle and the development of interurban computer hookups, and to extend the study of interurban relationships to include more specific business, profes-

---

41. An example of a valuable local study which does not make consistent use of such a context is Wheaton J. Lane, *From Indian Trial to Iron Horse, Travel and Transportation in New Jersey* (Princeton, 1939).
42. Allan R. Pred, *Urban Growth and the Circulation of Information: The United States System of Cities, 1790-1840* (Cambridge, 1973).
43. *Ibid.,* 142, 203-4.
44. *Ibid.,* 286.

sional, and social connections, such as systems of agents, partnerships, and branch operations; networks of scientists, lawyers, teachers, and ministers; and social links of marriage and common concerns between influential families.[45]

Pred's work demonstrates not just that Megalopolis was incipient from the time the nation began to take shape—that would be commonplace—but that the nation in fact took shape around this incipient Megalopolis. To analyze how this happened, to describe the ramifying spatial networks, intensifying circulations, and compounding of economic and demographic growth anchored upon this axis is fundamental to any understanding of the emergence of the United States as a geographic system.

There are encouraging signs of progress toward such an interpretation. I would point especially to the work emanating from the Regional Economic History Research Center of the Eleutherian Mills-Hagley Foundation in Wilmington, Delaware. The general recognition of what Thomas C. Cochran, Chairman of the Advisory Committee of the Center, calls a "geo-cultural" perspective, the focus of attention on the Northeastern United States, and a research emphasis on the development of regional systems represents the kind of fruitful cross-fertilization so long latent in American history and geography. Cochrane himself has shifted to an emphasis on this New York City-Philadelphia axis and the interdependence and complementarity of Northeastern seaboard cities.[46] And as a good example of how regional

---

45. Michael P. Conzen, "The Maturing Urban System in the United States, 1840-1910", *Annals of the Association of American Geographers* 67 (1977) 88-108. Examination of social and professional ties was begun many years ago by Michael Kraus, *Intercolonial Aspects of American Culture on the Eve of the Revolution, With Specal Reference to the Northern Towns* (New York, 1928). See also William S. Sacks, "Interurban Correspondents and the Development of a National Economy before the Revolution: New York as a Case Study", *New York History* 36 (1955) 320-55.

46. Thomas C. Cochran, "An Analytical View of Early American Business and Industry", in Joseph R. Frese and Jacob Judd, *Business Enterprise in Early New York* (Tarrytown, N.Y. 1979), 1-15, esp. p. 11 where he cites and clearly draws upon Pred; also Cochran, *Frontiers of Change: Early Industrialism in America* (New York, 1981), esp. p. 3 on "geocultural", and 7, 91, 112 on this region.

systems and hierarchies are formed and elaborated I would cite Burton Folsom's study of the emergence of Scranton as a regional center, how it drew talent and capital from earlier county towns nearby, how it developed its own civic consciousness, social leadership, and industrial-commercial system, how it created satellite coal towns in the Lackawanna Valley and extended its facilities of commerce, and how inexorable demands for growth capital brought the key industries and facilities of the entire area into the control of New York City interests.[47]

This kind of detailed examination of structure and function and key persons and corporations is fundamental to regional interpretation; it defines the skeleton, the essential organs, and the vital circulations, that give meaning to the external body of a region that we may delimit as a contiguous area upon our maps. And there is more to it than tracing the development of the spatial system, there are the alterations in the character of the places bound into that system, as Stuart Blumin's fine study of Kingston, New York, shows for a town that through no effort of its own found itself at a strategic junction of canal and river along that New York City-Scranton trunk line.[48] It thereby became part of a new human-use region and was profoundly affected. Furthermore, the development of new forms of transportation and new resources may alter the geography of circulation so that

47. Burton W. Folsom, "A Regional Analysis of Urban History: City Building in the Lackawanna Valley During Early Industrialization", *Working Papers from the Regional Economic History Research Center*, v.2 (Wilmington, Delaware, 1979), 71-100. Folsom's report is derived from his dissertation in history at the University of Pittsburgh, a department which added an historical geographer specializing on regional systems to its faculty a few years ago. Papers by David E. Dauer and by Diane Lindstrom in this same volume are further illustrations of regional analysis.
48. Stuart M. Blumin, *The Urban Threshold, Growth and Change in a Nineteenth Century American Community* (Chicago, 1976). See also his comments in support of the regional emphasis of the Wilmington research program: Blumin, "Economy and Society: Philadelphia and its Hinterland: A Commentary", *Working Papers from the Regional Economic History Research Center*, v. 2 (1979) 107-112.

areas previously quite separate are brought into close connection. Where these new links cut across major cultural boundaries a discordance may develop between the historic regions still vividly displayed in the vernacular landscape and the new regions created by functional systems of modern circulation. That sharp cultural divide between New York and Pennsylvania would eventually be crossed by several railroads, although because the traffic on these was largely coal the interregional impact was limited. And New York City increasingly bound a good part of western New England into its sphere of operations, but this was not an altogether new penetration of a cultural boundary for that part of Yankeedom had long been a major "catchment area" from which the city had drawn much leadership, professional talent, and manpower.

Even these brief examples are enough to hint at the need for a consistent historical examination of the development of these spatial systems so as to give geographic substance and more accurate definition to the emergence of a "Middle Atlantic" region, the "North," and an "American core area," and to the relationships of New York as a state and its varied subregions to such areas. At this point one can only say that these regional concepts so widely employed in our thinking are much too vague to be satisfying, and the persistence of such superficial pedagogic generalizations has contributed to the dismissal of regionalism as a dull ineffective tool.

I have touched upon some basic features pertinent to many of those standard regionalizations we reviewed at the outset: culture areas, human-use regions, megalopolis, a Middle Atlantic region or section. If my treatment has revealed something of the complexities of regionalism I hope that it may have stirred an interest in its possibilities rather than intimidated by its difficulties. I should hope that once we begin to discern the dynamics of regional development, to see structure and process, motivation and event at work in the continuous shaping of the geography of human affairs we can never again be content with the simple delimitations of regions as if they were static entities, whether blocs of states, human-use areas, or cultural surfaces, and certainly never waste our time searching for some final "best regional scheme" to suit all purposes. I should further hope that we would become attuned to see regions in the context of scale, to be aware that they are made up of parts and are themselves parts of something greater, and that we must develop a facility for shifting the scale of our perspective, for moving up and down in a hierarchy of areal generalizations. Thus, for example, that Philadelphia-New York City link is at once a set of two urban centers, two overlapping metropolitan regions, the central part of a larger complex interurban system, the bipolar anchor of westward penetration lines, the basic axis of a national network, and the continental hinge of a North Atlantic system. Each of these is an appropriate focus of study; the problem is to choose the scale best-suited for a particular purpose and to bear in mind the interrelatedness of all so as not to get hedged in by the limitations inherent in any one. The integrative nature of this regional approach should be an important attraction. Even a limited reconnaissance reveals how little explicit relation there is between the literatures devoted to individual cities, rivalries between cities, city and hinterland studies, rural studies, or between studies of colonies, states, and larger regions or sections. An historical analytic regional approach offers a means not just of binding these literatures more closely together, but a framework for a reformulation of the questions to be asked and a method for finding some answers.

All that I have suggested lies open to historians and geographers alike. We need each other, we need to borrow perspectives and methods from one another, we need to converge more closely upon some common themes. Broadly one may say that we have tended to focus on opposite ends of a common topic: the interpretation of how New York relates to the area or areas that both fields have asserted as having been of greatest importance in the overall patterns of American development. Most of the historical literature deals with the colonial period, and especially the late colonial era when New York and the Middle Colonies seemed to pre-figure the

character of the subsequent nation. After the Revolution this
critical area tends to dissolve into the broader sectionalism of
a North and East in apposition to a South and West. It is a
peculiarity of historiography that these colonial and national
periods tend to be two quite separate literatures by two sets
of historians. Most of the geographical literature deals with
tangible settlement and/or economic features of contemporary times and there have been some marked shifts in common regionalizations as areas or perceptions of areas have
changed over the past fifty years. It is a peculiarity of
American geography that the study of cultural and of
economic topics has increasingly produced two quite separate
literatures by two sets of geographers employing very different tools for different ends.

One would have to say that neither field has gotten very far
in defining at all clearly how the United States developed as a
geographic system and surface.[49] Until recently, historians
seem to have been handicapped by their obsession with
politics and the framing of their questions in terms of
political units, while especially recently geographers have
been handicapped by their obsession with economic patterns
of the current scene and the framing of their questions in
terms of geographic theory and public policies. One can cite
a few exceptions, of course. The sectionalism of the mature
Turner displayed a sure grasp of many of the complexities in
type and scale of the regional concept.[50] The culture areas of
Zelinsky, especially in the Northeast, are based on sensitivity
to a remarkable range of criteria and intimate field reconnaissance. That the most seminal study of regional systems
comes from a man, Allen Pred, who denies any real interest
in either history or regional geography *per se*, may be taken
as illustrating how far we are from having anything like the

---

49. For a possible approach and survey of pertinent geographic literature see D.
W. Meinig, ''The Continuous Shaping of America: A Prospectus for Geographers
and Historians,'' *American Historical Review*, 83 (1978) 1186-1217.
50. Turner, *The United States 1830-1850* (New York, 1935).

kind of regional historical geography I have been trying to envision and to suggest to you. The study of New York and its neighbors through the whole course of their history would provide a fine topic for such a literature. And my own limited experience leads me to suspect that the best reward for those who might undertake such work would not be the professional recognition of their contributions to an understanding of the United States, which I am certain would come, but their personal enrichment from the required development of an intimate sensitivity to the variety and qualities of the landscapes and localities of this handsome historic state.

"THE PROMISED SUNSHINE OF THE FUTURE" REFLECTIONS ON ECONOMIC GROWTH AND SOCIAL CHANGE IN POST-REVOLUTIONARY NEW YORK

MICHAEL KAMMEN

The audience at this symposium has been wonderfully benign and well-behaved. I only mention it because that might not have been the case in early national America, the era we have been examining. In those days the favorite form of public entertainment was melodrama; and we know that members of the audience often felt free to express themselves vocally throughout the performances. In one city, for example, a woman pleaded with the gamester to cease his shady behavior. In another a seated gent interrupted and objected to an assault on Coriolanus because "three on one" didn't seem to be a "fair fight." In New Orleans a boatman shouted at Othello, who was lamenting the loss of a handkerchief, "Why don't you blow your nose with your fingers and let the play go on."[1]

I find myself very much in sympathy with the purpose and focus of this symposium. To examine New York during the early national period is not only intrinsically interesting: it is historically appropriate as well. Nathaniel Hawthorne helped to explain why in an observation confided to his journal: "I wonder that we Americans love our country at all, it having no limits and no oneness; and when you try to make it a matter of the heart, everything falls away except one's native

---

1. Quoted in David Grimsted, *Melodrama Unveiled: American Theater and Culture 1800-1850* (Chicago, 1968), 60.

State.''[2] I do not insist that everyone in ante-bellum America would have agreed, but many did; so it behooves us to seek an understanding of New York's role in the young nation: how New Yorkers perceived themselves, how outsiders perceived the Empire State, and what kind of place it actually was becoming. I am disposed to argue that New York was *especially* distinctive in those days, and perhaps a majority of you are by now prepared to agree. The tricky matter, needless to say, is to specify the nature of that distinctiveness.[3]

I shall be striving toward that goal, and will confront it directly in the final sections of this paper. First, however, it is my assignment to respond to the three other papers that you have heard. I would like to do so mainly by way of augmentation and synthesis. Perhaps I can add a suggestion here and hypothesize an extra dimension there. I'll try. After addressing three segments of the paper to the broad subjects of my colleagues, I shall conclude by responding to two important yet rather elusive historical questions: How should we assess the impact of the revolutionary experience upon New York? And then, 41 years after its publication, what are we to make of that delightful and influential series of lectures by Dixon Ryan Fox, published as *Yankees and Yorkers*? As they used to say in the melodrama, more on those matters anon.

I

As I listened to Dr. Kline speak about an expanding state

---

2. Quoted in Barbara Novak, *Nature and Culture: American Landscape and Painting, 1825-1875* (New York, 1980), 223. Cf. James Madison's pejorative comment, made in 1775: "How different is the spirit of Virginia from that of N York?" Madison to William Bradford [early March 1775], *The Papers of James Madison*, eds. William T. Hutchinson and William M. E. Rachal (Chicago, 1962), I, 141.

3. In April 1974 the State University College at Oneonta sponsored a conference entitled "New York in the New Nation, 1777-1804." See also the proceedings of a conference held at Fordham University in November 1975 and published as an entire issue of *Early American Literature*, XI (Spring 1976). The theme is "Literature of the Revolution: The New York Scene [1765-1790]."

in the new nation, it struck me that a reality which most of us take for granted—namely, that New York is really two states—dates essentially from the period we have been examining. New Amsterdam and colonial New York City were quite different in character from early Long Island and the Hudson River Valley, of course; but the bases of our modern divergence (and conflicts) seem to have emerged with particular force between the age of Alexander Hamilton, let us say, and that of Martin Van Buren. In one sense Hamilton may have been rootless (I did not say ruthless); but in yet another sense one might insist that he had strong bonds to both New York City *and* to the Albany area. Moreover, as we know from his role in the great compromise of 1790, the biggest conflict for Hamilton lay not in the interests of downstate versus those of upstate, but between the economic imperatives of the nation as a whole and the attractiveness of political hegemony for New York State.[4]

I shall have more to say in a little while about upstate; but I want to begin by sharing with you my fascination with what happened to New York City during and after the American Revolution. It expanded, demographically and economically, at a stupendous rate. New York grew more rapidly and more consistently between 1790 and 1830 than any other city in the United States. Its emergence and pre-eminence as our leading seaport preceded by half a generation the completion of the Erie Canal. Between 1795 and 1810 New York's share of the coastal tonnage leaped from less than one-tenth to more than a quarter. By contrast, Boston's share slipped from half to less than one-third. If you examine a graph of bank capital available in New York, Philadelphia, Boston, and Baltimore between 1790 and 1826, you will find the four

---

4. See Jacob E. Cooke, "The Compromise of 1790," *William and Mary Quarterly*, 27 (Oct. 1970), 531, 533. I find it interesting and amusing to note that in 1883, after making a tour of the United States, Edward A. Freeman, the prominent British historian, asked: "would it not be a good thing to carry out a divorce between New York city and New York State?" *Some Impressions of the United States* (London, 1883), 247.

cities rather closely grouped and comparable until the years 1810-1813. During those few years New York's supply of bank capital zoomed upward so rapidly that no other city was remotely competitive thereafter.[5] Between 1790 and 1820 the population of Philadelphia grew by 147%, Boston's by 195%, but New York's by 295%.

These figures, and similar ones, are readily available and non-controversial. What fascinates me about them, and what seems problematic in certain respects, is their long range historical context—at first military and then political. In order to explain what I mean, I shall have to review a bit of chronology. After a while my chronology may seem to have more ups and downs then the Coney Island roller coster; but that is precisely the point. Between 1756 and 1797 the conditions for economic growth in New York were extraordinarily unstable.

Beginning in 1756, the French and Indian War brought an influx of British troops, fresh construction, and wealth to New York City. Lord Amherst arrived from Halifax in October 1758 and settled in for the winter. By mid-May 1759, however, Amherst had moved the army to Albany, en route to the conquest of Quebec. In November Amherst consolidated his gains and returned to New York City by way of Ticonderoga. In March, 1760, Amherst began to mobilize once again. Regiments were dispatched to various locations; and, as we all know, Amherst achieved a stupendous victory over the French at Montreal. Then back to New York City, of course, arriving on November 27, 1760, to an enthusiastic reception. Thereafter the war shifted to the Caribbean, and with it, in April 1761, a lot of troops, ships, and money. Amherst himself moved back and forth between Albany and Staten Island until 1763, when, following the Treaty of Paris,

---

5. See David T. Gilchrist, ed., *The Growth of the Seaport Cities, 1790-1825* (Charlottesville, Va., 1967), 30-31, 55-56; the graph appears on p. 112.

he returned to England.[6] The socio-economic impact of all this coming and going was neatly summarized by Anne Grant, the daughter of a British officer: "Money so easily got was as lightly spent and proved indeed ruinous to those who shared it; they being thus led to indulge in expensive habits, which continued after the means that supplied them were exhausted."[7]

For a decade after 1763, although New York remained nominal headquarters of the British commander-in-chief, relatively small detachments of troops were quartered in the city. Their presence seemed to be more of a political and economic nuisance than an advantage; and the local animosities are well known. New York City served as a nerve center for the much expanded British empire in North America—a switchboard for gathering information and disseminating orders. Residents of New York City, with a few exceptions, did not like the situation one bit and rejoiced in 1774 when the red-coats moved to Boston. Their happiness would be ephemeral, however. By the later part of 1775 fears that New York City would become the focal point of war caused a steady stream of departures. The arrival of Henry Clinton's royal fleet on February 4, 1776, caused panic and a hideous traffic jam. The population of New York City dropped from about 25,000 in 1775 to perhaps as few as twelve thousand at the moment of Independence. After the battle of Long Island, however, followed by Clinton's landing on Manhattan in September, occupying British soldiers, various sorts of camp followers, and loyalist refugees swelled the

---

6. Norreys J. O'Conor, *A Servant of the Crown in England and in North America, 1756-1761, based upon the papers of John Appy* . . . (New York, 1938), 32, 48-50, 137, 159; Lawrence Shaw Mayo, *Jeffrey Amherst: A Biography* (London, 1916), 113, 164-65, 190, 194, 213; John Shy, *Toward Lexington: The Role of the British Army in the Coming of the American Revolution* (Princeton, 1965), 96-98, 103, 107-109, 114-15.

7. Anne Grant, *Memoirs of an American Lady: With Sketches of Manners and Scenes in America* . . . (1809: Albany, 1876), 315.

city's population to more than 30,000.[8]

This extraordinary process of displacement during 1775-76 unleashed an immense number of problems and aggravated still others. How to collect taxes from wealthy inhabitants who had fled? How were landlords to pay their taxes when no rent was coming in? On September 21, 1776, an awesome fire destroyed 493 houses in New York City, ruined 500 others, and left a swath of desolation one mile long. On October 8 a second major fire occurred; the Hessians felt themselves at liberty to plunder the City; and health hazards suddenly became extemely problematic. The British made no effort to rebuild gutted areas, and a serious housing shortage developed. In 1776 there had been roughly 4,000 houses in the City. By 1786, three years after the British departure, there were perhaps 3,240.[9]

Until November 1783 New York City was ruled by military government. British residents paid no taxes of any kind, whether to clean the city, repair streets and pumps, or assist the poor. Abandoned stores were seized for use by the military. The British government supposedly paid rent for such facilities if the owners were Loyalists; and the British did subsidize those urban services normally paid for by taxes. Even so, support by the occupying power was never adequate because inflation swiftly raced out of control. The cost of provisions increased by about 800%. A group of prominent citizens tried to take responsibility for social welfare, but met with small success. As Alexander Hamilton put it in 1777, "New York has been stripped extremely bare." Between

---

8. Bernard Mason, *The Road to Independence: The Revolutionary Movement in New York, 1773-1777* (Lexington, Ky., 1966), 78-79, 103, 106, 172, 191; Bruce Bliven, Jr., *Under the Guns: New York, 1775-1776* (New York, 1972), 121, 178; William B. Willcox, *Portrait of a General: Sir Henry Clinton in the War of Independence* (New York, 1964), 69-70; Bruce M. Wilkenfeld, "Revolutionary New York, 1776," in Milton M. Klein, ed., *New York: The Centennial Years, 1676-1976* (Port Washington, N. Y., 1976), 43-72.

9. Mason, *op. cit.*, 196; Wilbur C. Abbott, *New York in the American Revolution* (New York, 1929), 187-88, 194-95, 199, 206-17, 246; Sidney I. Pomerantz, *New York: An American City, 1783-1803* (New York, 1938), 226-27, 230-31.

1781 and 1783, in fact, the British cut down every tree in the
New York City area for fuel. Manhattan was cleared from
end to end, so that thickets and young saplings were just
beginning to grow back by 1819.[10]

By the close of 1781 most Americans in New York felt
reasonably certain that the British forces would have to
withdraw, making way for the patriots to return. Loyalists
departed in phases, however: 7,000 sailing in April, and
another 8,000 refugees in September 1783. Not until
November, though, did the British officially evacuate—giving up their final foothold in what became the thirteen
original states. Despite the understandable exuberance of the
ten or twelve thousand souls who remained, New York City
was thrown into turmoil. A large number of auctions took
place, usually to the benefit of those who stayed. More property (belonging to military personnel as well as to Loyalist
refugees) changed hands in less time than at any other point
in New York's history. Patriots who had fled in 1776 returned to find their property legally in the hands of former
neighbors and friends. Inadequate police protection encouraged rampant lawlessness; and to make matters worse,
rents and prices remained high throughout 1784.[11]

During the next five years New York City made a gradual
but nonetheless remarkable recovery. Markets were rebuilt,
houses were constructed to accommodate new immigrants
from Ireland, Connecticut, and the whole Hudson Valley.
The population leaped from about 12,000 late in 1783 to
more than 23,000 by 1786, 33,000 in 1790, and 60,000 by

10. I. N. Phelps Stokes, *The Iconography of Manhattan Island, 1498-1909* (New
York, 1915-28), I, 327-28, 333-34; Oscar T. Barck, Jr., *New York City During the
War for Independence* (New York, 1931); Alexander Hamilton to Horatio Gates,
Nov. 13, 1777, in Harold C. Syrett, ed., *The Papers of Alexander Hamilton* (New
York, 1961), I, 362; Frances Wright, *Views of Society and Manners in America,*
ed. Paul R. Baker (Cambridge, Mass., 1963), 15.
11. Abbott, *New York in the Revolution,* 141-69, 262-63, 269-75, 279; Hugh
Hastings, comp., *Public Papers of George Clinton* (Albany, 1904), VIII, 257-61,
269-78, 282-85, 288-89, 293-318; Pomerantz, *op. cit.,* 19-22, 76, 147-48; and
Papers of James Madison, II, 182.

1800. Fourteen new churches had appeared by 1800, most notably the handsome reincarnation of Trinity Church (1788-90), whose imposing steeple now dominated the metropolis.[12]

By 1788-89 New York was obviously flourishing once again. As a French visitor remarked, "the activity which reigns on all sides announces the prosperity of the future. Everywhere streets are being widened and extended. Elegant buildings in the English style are replacing the gabled Dutch houses, of which there are some still left."[13] It is symbolic, perhaps, that Trinity's rebuilding coincided with the establishment of New York City as the nation's capital, a decision that was understood to be provisional at the time, but one that New Yorkers hoped would become permanent. Prominent physicians proclaimed the healthfulness of the City's climate; on June 24, 1789, the *Gazette of the United States* announced that during the Congressional session of almost three months duration only one member had become ill. Being the national capital brought prestige as well as profits.[14]

The New York delegation accordingly maneuvered and conspired during the spring of 1790 to prevent a temporary move to Philadelphia followed by permanent relocation on the banks of the Potomac; but to no avail. Alexander Hamilton cared more about federal assumption of state debts than he did about keeping the capital in New York. South Carolina and Maryland shifted their support to the Pennsylvania-Virginia coalition; and New York lost the battle.[15] On August 12, 1790, the Senate held its final session

12. Pomerantz, *op. cit.*, 167-200, 237-96; E. Wilder Spaulding, *New York in the Critical Period, 1783-1789* (New York, 1932), 12, 18; Thomas C. Cochran, *New York in the Confederation: An Economic Study* (Philadelphia, 1932) 151, 165.

13. J. P. Brissot de Warville, *New Travels in the United States of America, 1788*, ed. Durand Echeverria (Cambridge, Mass., 1964), 145.

14. *Ibid.*, 140-41; Thomas E. V. Smith, *The City of New York in the Year of Washington's Inauguration, 1789* (New York, 1889), 6-7, 88.

15. Cooke, *loc. cit.*, 528-31, 533, 536; Charles A. Beard, ed., *The Journal of William Maclay* (New York, 1927), 134, 161-62, 330-31.

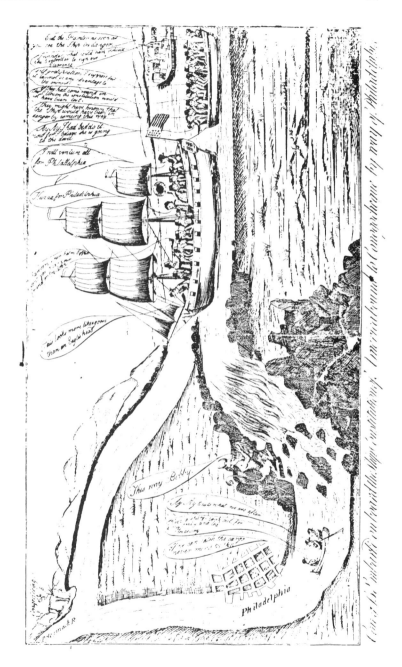

1. "Congress Embark'd on board the Ship Constitution . . . by Way of Philadelphia," *courtesy of the Historical Society of Pennsylvania.*

2. "Robert Morris Moves the Seat of Government to Philadelphia,"
courtesy of the American Antiquarian Society.

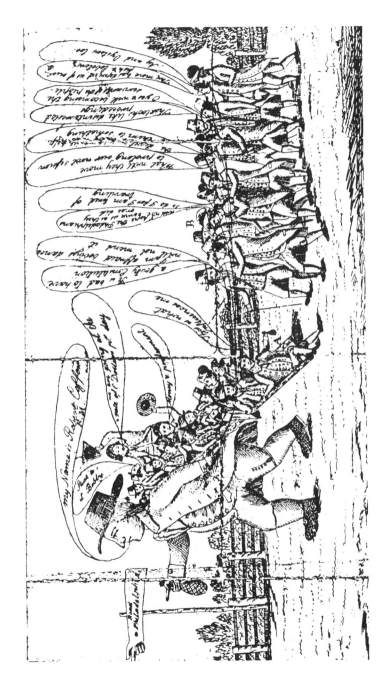

3. "View of Congress on the Road to Philadelphia," *courtesy of the New York Historical Society.*

there; and on the 28th George Washington entertained the governor, the mayor, and the city corporation in order "to express his great reluctance at leaving the city, and those citizens who had taken so much pains to treat him, not only with dignified respect, but with reverence and esteem." On August 30 the President departed for Philadelphia by barge.[16] (Figures 1, 2 and 3)

Although the iconography of this event is perhaps peripheral to our focus, it is noteworthy that contemporary cartoons blamed Robert Morris as the chief villain behind the move. Notice that in two of the three illustrations the devil is depicted as leading the way—in one by land and in another by water. In the third there is no devil visible, just Robert Morris himself, larger than life, hauling a load of corrupt retainers. The irony in all of this, needless to say, involves much more than the long-standing commerical rivalry between Philadelphia and New York. In 1788 Robert Morris had bought a vast amount of land east of the Genesee River from Oliver Phelps and Nathaniel Gorham, and then sold half of it at a fat profit to a group of English capitalists. Encouraged by that lucrative transaction, Morris bought land west of the Genesee and in 1792-93 sold most of it to Theophile Cazenove, now a representative of the six Dutch banking houses that later organized as the Holland Land Company. This last sale comprised 3.3 million acres, a vast portion of western New York. Is it any wonder the inhabitants resented Robert Morris so much?

What *is* central to our focus, and intrigues me, is that the apprehensions of New Yorkers about the consequences of the move to Philadelphia turned out to be utterly unjustified.

---

16. *The New-York Journal, & Patriotic Register,* August 31, 1790. This newspaper maintained a constant, cynical and bitter commentary on the move. See August 10, 13 and 24; September 3, 21, and 28; October 26; November 4, 8, 11, 15, 18, 22 and 25; and December 6, 1790.

Even allowing for touches of hyperbole, people feared that New York would become less innovative and progressive, more provincial, depopulated, "a wilderness again, peopled with wolves." Philip Freneau worried about the paving problem, sure that New York's streets "will now be neglected and nasty as ever." Except for the $50,000 that had been spent to decorate Federal Hall, it is difficult to see what, if anything, New York lost in economic terms. Anti-Federalists like Theodorus Bailey of Dutchess County even said "good riddance"; and many others believed that the presence of government raised rents, inflated prices, stimulated luxurious living and corrupted morals. Those who did resent the move would have found consolation in a letter that Abigail Adams sent to her daughter on November 21, 1790: "If New York wanted any revenge for the removal, the citizens might be glutted if they would come here [to Philadelphia], where every article has become almost double in price, and where it is not possible for Congress, and the appendages, to be half as well accommodated for a long time." The Vice President's wife had been much happier in New York City.[17]

If New York was relatively unaffected (and even unconcerned) about losing the national capital in 1790, the city seems to have been indifferent or else resigned to the incredibly casual decision, made in 1797, to move the state capital to Albany. The reasons for the move, and for its timing, are not at all clear;[18] but there is a kernel of truth in the cynical explanation provided by Sir Augustus John Foster,

---

17. Frank Monaghan and Marvin Lowenthal, *This Was New York, the Nation's Capital in 1789* (New York, 1943), 30, 281-82; Alfred F. Young, *The Democratic Republicans of New York: The Origins, 1763-1797* (Chapel Hill, 1967), 183-85; Charles Francis Adams, ed., *Letters of Mrs. Adams, the Wife of John Adams* (3rd ed.: Boston, 1841), II, 209.

18. See Codman Hislop, *Albany: Dutch, English, and American* (Albany, 1936), 228-34; Arthur J. Weise, *The History of the City of Albany, New York . . .* (Albany, 1884), 424-27. Curiously enough *The Diary of Elihu Hubbard Smith (1771-1798)*, ed. by James E. Cronin (Philadelphia, 1973) never refers to the move. Smith was a native of Albany, lived there in 1797-98, and kept an extensive journal with frequent reference to public events.

Secretary of the British Legation in Washington from 1805 until 1807:

> In conformity with the pettyfogging jealousy towards the real capital that exists in many other parts of the United States, New York like Pennsylvania, is forced to fix the seat of government in a small town, Albany, where the rustic legislators may not be subject to have their feelings wounded by seeing fine horses, equipages or dress, or any other outward and visible mark of superiority of their own. One would have supposed that such great politicians might have preferred to live in the centre of arts and sciences, trade and commerce, where minds of every description meet and improve one another, by the mutual interchange of ideas, and the polish of social life... The poor commonplace passions of envy jealousy and parsimony, as well as a certain want of concern for the dignity of government, lead the other way, while the paltry argument about a central spot being necessary, as if the whole state were a wheel, is opposed by the majority to any advantage of humanization or instruction to be derived from the chief members of the state residing in a large city.[19]

When Frances Wright toured throughout New York in 1819 she encountered the expectation that "the government will soon have to travel in search of the centre of the republic," and learned that "newborn Utica already aspires to be the capital of the state, and in a few years it probably will be so . . . . The young western counties are such stout and imperious children that it will soon be found necessary to consult their interests."[20]

---

19. Richard Beale Davis, ed., *Jeffersonian America: Notes on the United States of America Collected in the Years 1805-6-7 and 11-12 by Sir Augustus John Foster, Bart.* (San Marino, Ca., 1954), 228.
20. Wright, *op. cit.,* 79, 95.

If I may now summarize the implications of what I have been describing, New York City between 1757 and 1797 underwent an extraordinary series of demographic expansions and contractions; it literally changed hands twice (in 1776 and 1783); and then lost both the national as well as the state capital in 1790 and 1797.[21] The public spending that accompanies military importance came and went. The prestige and affluence that accompany political importance came and went. A prolonged series of severe housing shortages was endured. Several disastrous fires occurred. More often than not New York served as a point of departure rather than a beacon of welcome.

If one looks at some roughly comparable instances in history, the socio-economic consequences have been disastrous: when the papacy returned from Avignon to Rome in 1378, Avignon shrivelled. When the imperial capital of Japan moved from Kyoto to Tokyo in 1868, Kyoto diminished considerably in significance. Before the Russian capital was moved in 1918, St. Petersburg was much larger than Moscow; now it is only half as large.[22]

Although New York failed twice to become and remain what anthropologists call a "court city," it nevertheless emerged in the early nineteenth century as the premier urban site of the entire United States. As a French visitor put it in October 1794, "New York is less citified than Philadelphia, but the bustle of trade is far greater."[23] Allan R. Pred has called New York during this era "the principal node of the nation's information circulation system"; and indeed, in

---

21. It may be symptomatic that James Rivington suffered bankruptcy in New York in 1760 and again in 1797. Between 1784 and 1793 financial difficulties prevented Rivington from issuing a single book. See Leroy Hewlett, "James Rivington, Tory Printer," in David Kaser, ed., *Books in America's Past: Essays Honoring Rudolph H. Gjelsness* (Charlottesville, 1966), 166-93.

22. See especially James H. Bater, *St. Petersburg: Industrialization and Change* (London, 1976), especially chapters 6 and 7, "The Twilight of the Imperial City" and "The Dimensions of Change."

23. Kenneth and Anna Roberts, eds., *Moreau de St. Méry's American Journey* [1793-1798], (Garden City, N. Y., 1947), 146.

1794 the first anthology of American poetry, called *The Co-lumbian Muse,* was published there. Somehow, the oldest city in the United States, founded in 1626, had become re-invigorated. If it was less of a community, and had a vaguer sense of identity than Boston, Philadelphia, Baltimore and Charleston, it at least enjoyed the benefits of a more accessi-ble social structure.[24] New York was open to talent, and one of the neglected aspects of its history during these years in-volves the bold and skillful entrepreneurial types who were attracted to it, ranging from Duncan Phyfe, the fabulous fur-niture maker, to William Edwards, grandson of the sermonic Jonathan, and founder of the hide and leather industry in the United States.

Visitors commented most frequently about New York's superb location. The secretary to Britain's new minister to the United States marveled in 1791 at the "situation" of New York: "The wit of man could not have contrived one more admirably adapted to the purpose of commerce. It is certainly favored to be the first city in North America, and this superiority it will most assuredly retain whatever other spot be made the seat of government."[25] Brissot de Warville, who visited New York in 1788, was equally impressed by New York's advantageous location. He noted that it had become "both the port of export for the products of Con-necticut and New Jersey and also the center for the distribu-tion to these states of all the products of Europe and the East Indies." It also impressed him that "the soundness of this city's finances and its promptness in paying the interest on its debt contribute greatly toward the stability of its paper

---

24. See Allan R. Pred, *Urban Growth and the Circulation of Information: The United States System of Cities, 1790-1840* (Cambridge, Mass., 1973), 142, 203-04; Martin B. Green, *Cities of Light and Sons of the Morning: A Cultural Psychology for an Age of Revolution* (Boston, 1972), 222.

25. S. W. Jackman, ed., "A Young Englishman Reports on the New Nation: Ed-ward Thornton to James Bland Burges, 1791-1793," *William and Mary Quarter-ly,* 18 (Jan. 1961), 91. The letter was written from Philadelphia on Oct. 31, 1791.

money . . . .''[26]

Modern scholars interested in urban change and economic growth have offered a cluster of reasons why New York blossomed so much more rapidly than any other American city in this era: (1) it was the most attractive city to foreign immigrants; (2) the population of its hinterland grew at an amazing rate; (3) between 1799 and 1829 New York strengthened the physical bonds between its hinterland and port city by permitting 253 incorporations for the construction of turnpikes and 70 for bridge companies; (4) perceiving, even anticipating New York's meteoric rise, businessmen made decisions and commitments that accelerated economic growth, such as the early development of more specialized commercial institutions. The securities market, for example, was centered in the city by 1817 with the formation of a Board of Brokers. Thereafter New York's Stock Exchange offered the broadest market for securities in the United States. My point is that in addition to such tangibles as a fine harbor and rapid demographic growth, New York achieved a distinctive state of mind—or determination, if you will—in these years. Joseph Dorfman argued in 1966 that ''It is this vision of the city as the coming integrated cosmopolis which runs through the writings of New Yorkers during the whole period and which is largely absent in the works of residents of the other major cities.''[27]

II

Professor Meinig's lucid presentation concerning New York and its neighbors stimulates me to call attention to three related aspects of New York's distinctiveness during the post-revolutionary era. The first involves a simple suggestion

---

26. Brissot de Warville, *op. cit.,* 140-42, 150-51.
27. Gilchrist, ed., *op. cit.,* 30-33, 37, 56, 60, 69-71, 73-75, 90, 114-15, 127, 130-31. Dorfman's statement appears on p. 157. See also Gary B. Nash, *The Urban Crucible: Political Consciousness and the Origins of the American Revolution* (Cambridge, Mass., 1979).

that we look more systematically at the observations of visitors—those from other states as well as from abroad. Some of these will do little more than document what we already know, as when Sir Augustus Foster tells us during the Jeffersonian era that he "cannot conceive a finer situation for a commercial town than that of New York," and that "fortunes were rapidly made by mercantile speculations from this great port.'[28]

Others, regardless of whether we agree or not, indicate that contemporaries regarded New York as unique. Moreau de St. Méry, for example, believed that "the population of New York has a physiognomy of its own, due to its descent from the ancient Dutch and the ancient English." Many visitors were impressed by the quality of private homes in New York State. Such phrases as "neat white dwellings" and "well-finished houses" appear again and again.[29] On the other hand, one rarely finds any consensus in their judgments of particular towns. In 1793 John Heckewelder found Schenectady "striking to the Eye," whereas Timothy Dwight, the condescending president of Yale College, considered the architecture of Schenectady "uncouth" and believed that "the morals of the inhabitants, particularly of the inferior classes, are extensively upon a low scale."[30]

In the spring of 1791, Thomas Jefferson and James Madison journeyed through upstate New York, then across Vermont, down the Connecticut River Valley, and back to New York City by way of Long Island. It is impressive that Jefferson, who had just returned from six years of extensive travel in Europe, declared that "Lake George is, without comparison, the most beautiful water I ever saw . . . ." Always intrigued by climate, Jefferson complained that the weather during his trip had been "sultry and hot." On

28. Davis, ed., *op. cit.*, 293-96; Wright, *op. cit.*, 15.
29. Roberts, ed., *op. cit.*, 156; Wright, *op. cit.*, 13-14, 95.
30. Paul A. W. Wallace, ed., *Thirty Thousand Miles with John Heckewelder* (Pittsburgh, 1958), 297-98; Timothy Dwight, *Travels in New England and New York*, ed. Barbara Miller Solomon (Cambridge, Mass., 1969), II, 340.

balance, he concluded, "I find nothing anywhere else, in point of climate, which Virginia need envy to any part of the world. Here [meaning upstate New York; he was writing from Lake Champlain] they are locked up in snow and ice for six months. Spring and autumn, which make a paradise of our country, are rigorous winter with them; and a tropical summer breaks on them all at once."[31]

More significant, however, was Frances Wright's observation in 1821 that New York seemed especially supportive of internal improvements, notably "in the clearing of rivers, making roads and canals, and promoting other works of extensive utility . . . . The progress of the New York state during the last thirty years is truly astonishing. Within this period, her population has more than quadrupled, and the value of property more than doubled. She has subdued the forest from Hudson to Erie and the Canadian frontier, and is now perfecting the navigation of all her great waters and connecting them with each other."[32] The realities were somewhat more complicated than Wright understood, however.

In order to encourage manufacturing, for example, the legislature passed a five year General Incorporation Statute in 1811. It was particularly designed to encourage the construction of textile mills that would produce various types of thread for household weaving. Entrepreneurs favored such comprehensive legislation because it enabled them to seek incorporation without having to relate their proposed business to a narrow definition of public service, and because its inexpensive legal procedures required no special lobbying to pass individual charters. The state preferred this sort of act because manufacturing corporations—such as textile production, brewing, glass-making, and the metal trades (after

31. Thomas Jefferson to Martha Jefferson Randolph, May 31, 1791, in Paul Leicester Ford, ed., *The Works of Thomas Jefferson* (New York, 1904), VI, 264-65. See also Dumas Malone, *Jefferson and the Rights of Man* (Boston, 1951), 359-63.
32. Wright, *op. cit.*, 196-97.

about 1820)—were politically non-controversial. By contrast—and here is where Frances Wright did not comprehend
the complexity of the situation—New York's legislature
never incorporated shipbuilders, tanners of shoe leather, or
canal boat transportation companies because such enterprises
traditionally had been full liability companies and highly
competitive. In 1821 New York established the 1811 General
Incorporation Statute on a permanent basis.[33] By that time,
despite the depression of 1819, prosperity was *not* "just
around the corner." Owing to selective public intervention,
prosperity had long since arrived.

A second point pertaining to New York's distinctiveness
during this period is exceedingly obvious: namely, that New
York was more directly involved in the War of 1812 than
most other states, and hence much more affected. The war
had significant economic consequences, hastened the
development of transportation routes across the state
(especially those leading to Lakes Erie and Ontario), and
enhanced the military and naval expertise among New
York's young men. These trends may be traced quite clearly
through the careers of Solomon Van Rensselaer, Stephen Van
Rensselaer and others.[34]

My third point is equally straightforward, but apparently
not at all obvious because I do not believe it has been made.
We all know that the so-called Second Great Awakening
swept the mid-Atlantic and southern frontiers during the
earliest years of the nineteenth century. It even displayed
manifestations at New England colleges, where an enthusiasm for foreign missions developed. The impact of this
evangelical movement was so pervasive that Henry May ends

---

33. See Ronald E. Seavoy, "Laws to Encourage Manufacturing: New York Policy
and the 1811 General Incorporation Statute," *Business History Review*, 46
(Spring 1972), 85-95; Beatrice G. Reubens, "State Financing of Private Enterprise
in Early New York" (unpub. PhD dissertation, Columbia University, 1960).

34. It should be noted that the prolonged war in Europe, 1792-1815, caused
wheat and other grain prices to soar, a great boon for the farmers of New York.
See also Allan S. Everest, *The War of 1812 in the Champlain Valley* (Syracuse,
1981).

his recent account of the Enlightenment in America at 1800. So far as May is concerned, a major transformation took place in that year.

We also know, or think we know, that upstate New York was the "burned-over district"; but Whitney R. Cross has perpetrated a slight deception by sub-titling his well-known work *The Social and Intellectual History of Enthusiastic Religion in Western New York, 1800-1850.* In reality, though, and this is what helps to make New York so distinctive in the period we are examining, revivals on a significant scale did not begin to occur in the state until the mid and later 1820s. New York just plain did not experience the great evangelical revival of the first quarter of the nineteenth century. Instead, the state remained as godless and indifferent as it had been throughout most of the eighteenth century; and it was perceived as such by visitors to New York City, Long Island, and the Hudson River Valley.[35]

III

Dr. Siles's thorough study of activities by Phelps and Gorham in the Genesee region also prompts me to emphasize three facets of New York's early entrepreneurial history. (I am not usually such a strict "trinitarian"; but perhaps I am reacting to Union's excessively latitudinarian

---

35. The dates are equally misleading in the subtitle of Paul E. Johnson's well-regarded *A Shopkeeper's Millennium: Society and Revivals in Rochester New York, 1815-1837* (New York, 1978), a book primarily about the Rochester revival of 1830-31. In *Cradle of the Middle Class: The Family in Oneida County, New York, 1790-1865* (Cambridge, England, 1981), Mary P. Ryan notes minor revivals that occurred in the Utica area during 1814 and 1819; but the *Western Recorder,* an evangelical journal, did not appear until 1824, and the first major revival came in 1830-32 (see pp. 60, 75, 79). See also Dixon Ryan Fox, "The Protestant Counter-Reformation in America," *New York History,* 16 (Jan. 1935), 24-26, 28, 30. Harry F. Jackson's *Scholar in the Wilderness: Frances Adrian Van der Kemp* (Syracuse, 1963), treats an enlightened scholar during his long career in Oneida County, 1788-1829. Van der Kemp's role as a clergyman seems to have been incidental to his activities as translator, amateur geologist, historian and activist in public life.

origins!)

The first of my suggestions might be considered a revisionist addendum to David Maldwyn Ellis's essay on "The Rise of the Empire State, 1790-1820."[36] In order to *become* the Empire State, between about 1785 and 1810 New York had to undergo a process of "de-colonization." What I am referring to is a phenomenon that Dr. Kline and Professor Meinig each touched upon casually in their papers: namely, the immense amount of land in post-revolutionary New York that was owned by, shall we say, "outsiders." The Commonwealth of Massachusetts controlled six million acres. Phelps, who came from Connecticut, and Gorham, who came from Boston, determined the destiny of the vast Genesee country, just about the choicest land in western New York. They, in turn, sold vast chunks of real estate to Robert Morris. William Bingham of Philadelphia also owned a large stretch along the southern tier, including the eventual site of Binghamton (which is named in his honor even though he did nothing to develop it). (Figure 4) The blatant fact of the matter is that speculators in New England, Philadelphia and Baltimore owned some mighty large and fine parcels of land in upstate New York. Then add an international dimension: James Le Ray de Chaumont of Paris, who owned much of Jefferson County; Baron von Steuben, who held 16,000 acres; Sir William Pulteney and his associates, who bought much of Robert Morris's holdings; and then, above all, the Holland Land Company, a Dutch conglomerate that owned 3.3 million acres in western New York (centering on Batavia).[37]

---

36. *New York History,* 56 (Jan. 1975), 5-27.

37. Barbara A. Chernow, "Robert Morris: Land Speculator, 1790-1801" (unpub. PhD diss., Columbia University, 1978); Robert C. Alberts, *The Golden Voyage: The Life and Times of William Bingham, 1752-1804* (Boston, 1969), 115, 364; William Chazanof, *Joseph Ellicott and the Holland Land Company: The Opening of Western New York* (Syracuse, 1970); Horst Dippel, "German Emigration to the Genesee Country in 1792: An Episode in German-American Migration," in *Germany and America: Essays on Problems of International Relations and Immigration,* ed. by Hans L. Trefousse (New York, 1980), 161-69.

4. ''Binghamton: A view of Court Street from the Chenango Bridge to the Court House, taken June 4, 1810'' *(watercolor) by George Park, courtesy of the Broome County Historical Society.*

The potential list of names in this context is considerable: Jeremiah Halsey and Edward Ward (the Connecticut Gore), David Parish, Theophile Cazenove, and so on. My point, as I have already indicated, is a simple one. Before New York could become "imperial," it had to undergo a complex process of de-colonization—complex for many reasons, not least of which was the controversial question of whether land owned by non-residents could be taxed.

A second comment occurs to me. Dr. Siles's paper quite properly calls our attention to the importance of central planning and collective efforts in appreciating the economic development of upstate New York. Although I am impressed by the validity of that emphasis, I am also impressed by the role of small individual entrepreneurs—remarkable virtuosi whose stories in many instances have never been properly told. Take as just one illustration the case of Talmadge Edwards, a name, I suspect, that means absolutely nothing to most of you. Born in northern England in 1747, he learned the trade of leather dresser as a teenager. In about 1770 he emigrated to the colonies, initially to Rhode Island, but subsequently to Beekman's Precinct in Dutchess County, New York, where he found work in his trade. After serving in the county militia (on the patriot side) during the Revolution, he moved in 1783 to Johnstown, in Fulton County, where Indians and whites brought furs to the trading posts. In 1784 he bought land in Johnstown, opened a general store, but also continued to work as a leather dresser. In 1809 a small group of unsuccessful glove manufacturers at nearby Kingsboro invited Edwards to teach his method of leather-tanning to their glovemakers. Edwards then sensed the existence of a broader market, and hence a larger opportunity, than simply the Johnstown-Kingsboro area. So he persuaded country girls to come to his tannery in order to cut out gloves, which would then be sent to farmers' wives for sewing and completion. In 1810 Edwards took dozens of pairs to Albany in order to restock (by barter) his general store with merchandise. Along the way, however, he sold his stock of gloves. These modest beginnings in 1809-10 marked nothing less than the start of the glove and mitten industry in the United States. In addition to organizing the manufacture of gloves, Edwards then improved the process of tanning glove leather. He developed the "oil-tan" method for preparing buckskin, a process that was still in use a century after his death in 1821.

The third point that I would like to make in conjunction with Dr. Siles's paper pertains to the gradual emergence during these decades of scientific agriculture. When Frances Wright visited the Genesee district in August, 1819, she wrote rapturously that "agriculture here assumes her most cheerful aspect, and . . . all her ancient classic dignity." Despite Wright's emphasis upon the virtuous yeoman and the continuity of millennia, changes had been in the making ever since Crèvecoeur exchanged bushels of seeds and information about potatoes with Thomas Jefferson in 1784. Crèvecoeur was not merely the author of *Letters from an American Farmer* (1782), but of the *Journey into Northern Pennsylvania and the State of New York* (1801) as well; and in the later publication his message proclaimed that a new society would emerge as a result of agricultural development in the wilderness.[38]

The genesis of agricultural societies in New York is sufficiently well known and requires no repetition here. A Society for Promoting Agriculture, Arts and Manufacturing was founded in 1791, chartered by the legislature in 1793, and reorganized in 1804. Its leaders were gentlemen farmers from the elite, to be sure—the likes of Robert R. Livingston, John Jay, and Samuel Mitchell—but when the first New York State fair took place at Cooperstown in 1817, and when a State Board of Agriculture came into existence in 1820 (with 26 counties represented), one can properly say that the

---

38. Wright, *op. cit.,* 99; Merrill D. Peterson, *Thomas Jefferson and the New Nation* (New York, 1970), 293; Richard Slotkin, *Regeneration Through Violence: The Mythology of the American Frontier, 1600-1860* (Middletown, Conn., 1973), 336-37.

agrarian enlightenment had undergone Phase I of its democratization. The correspondence between DeWitt Clinton and Francis Adrian Van der Kemp (1812-1828) devotes a great deal of space to exchanging information on scientific agriculture; and when Jesse Buel had hatched his nest-egg as printer to the State of New York (1814-20), he "retired" in order to devote himself to agricultural education. His innovations made his farm west of Albany a showplace. In 1822 he became recording secretary to the State Board of Agriculture; and a year later, when he won election to the New York Assembly, he became the leading spokesman in the state for agricultural improvement, a role he continued to perform until his death in 1839. By that time the proliferation of agricultural journals had made the new techniques accessible to farmers throughout the state.[39]

IV

During the 1970s it became commonplace for historians to assert that the peculiar conditions of life in colonial New York anticipated what the United States as a whole would be like during the nineteenth century. The time has come, perhaps, to convert that assertion into a question, a hypothesis to be tested. If we ask in an open-minded way, "what impact did the American Revolution have upon New York?", we find not merely the absence of a consensus among scholars, but a curiously narrow range of response: essentially, that *democratization* was either a cause of the Revolution (e.g., Carl Becker and Gary Nash), or an accom-

---

39. Donald B. Marti, "Early Agricultural Societies in New York: The Foundations of Improvement," *New York History*, 48 (Oct. 1967), 313-31; Vivian C. Hopkins, "The Dutch Records of New York: Francis Adrian Van der Kemp and DeWitt Clinton," *ibid.*, 43 (Oct. 1962), 385-99; Ulysses P. Hedrick, "What Farmers Read in Western New York, 1800-1850," *ibid.*, 17 (1936), 281-89; Harry J. Carman, ed., *Jesse Buel, Agricultural Reformer* (New York, 1947); Peter H. Cousins, *Hog Plow and Sith: Cultural Aspects of Early Agricultural Technology* (Dearborn, Mich., 1973).

paniment to it (e.g., Merrill Jensen and Jackson Turner Main), or else a consequence of it (e.g., J. Franklin Jameson and Dixon Ryan Fox). Much as I respect the work of all those historians, the problem of "impact" must be vastly more complex than the monolithic matter of democratization. Fox, for example, tells us that by 1821 the Federalists became thoroughly discredited in New York and consequently lost high office and power in the state forever.[40] What I find so striking, however, is that New York became attractive to poor immigrants at least 25 years before it supposedly underwent "democratization". Moreover, just to complicate matters even further, large parts of New York seem to have undergone democratization ahead of schedule, so to speak; that is, before such economic conditions as the broad distribution of property made political and social democratization inevitable.

I believe that we might benefit immensely at this point from a comparative perspective, and more particularly from a brilliant little book by Tulio Halperín-Donghi entitled *The Aftermath of Revolution in Latin America* (New York, 1973). Just a glance at the issues he highlights will demonstrate that our customary focus has been surprisingly limited. Because of constraints on time and space here, I shall call your attention to four phenomena discussed by Halperín-Donghi, and interpolate for each one the stark contrast with New York. (Needless to say, a similar exercise needs to be performed for the United States as a whole.)

1. Halperín-Donghi asks why the changes which those leaders responsible for independence expected to occur immediately were delayed for almost 50 years. Why was the advent of liberalism so retarded, and the post-revolutionary order so static? (pp. viii, 140) By contrast, changes occurred rapidly in New York, the post-revolutionary order was quite

---

40. Fox, *The Decline of Aristocracy in the Politics of New York, 1801-1840* (2nd ed.: New York, 1965), 266.

fluid, the suffrage was extended, and the state constitution liberalized in 1821.

2. Militarization did not disappear at the end of the Latin American wars of independence. An extended period of disorder increased the army's influence and made it an alternative basis for political power and governance (pp. 18, 21, 43). In New York and the United States, of course, military influence waned rapidly, especially during the Jeffersonian era.

3. In Latin America societies which professed to support equality actually preserved quite zealously a state of social inequality. The equilibrium of the colonial caste system was much less affected by the Revolutions than many contemporaries would have admitted (pp. 27, 31, 115-16). Here the contrast with post-revolutionary New York is admittedly less compelling. Thomas Cochran concluded his study of *New York in the Confederation* (1932) by observing that "the State land system was administered in favor of the large grantees just as the British had been. All in all, the Revolution may be said to have had a comparatively small social effect in New York" (p. 182). If we look beyond the 1780s, however, we find that the confiscation of large Tory estates did make a gradual difference, that new economic opportunities did open up for "mechanics" and the proletariat, that public schools and charities not only developed but had a positive effect, and, that by the early 1800s schemes to assist the poverty-stricken began to appear.[41]

4. Halperín-Donghi demonstrates that a short-lived prosperity gave way to economic ruin after 1810. Britian over-

---

41. See Howard B. Rock, *Artisans of the New Republic: The Tradesmen of New York City in the Age of Jefferson* (New York, 1979); Drew R. McCoy, *The Elusive Republic: Political Economy in Jeffersonian America* (Chapel Hill, N. C., 1980), 117-18, 225; Raymond A. Mohl, *Poverty in New York, 1783-1825* (New York, 1971); Alexander C. Flick, ed., *The American Revolution in New York: Its Political, Social and Economic Significance* (2nd ed.: Port Washington, N. Y., 1967), 233, 235; and Carl F. Kaestle, *The Evolution of an Urban School System: New York City, 1750-1850* (Cambridge, Mass., 1973).

whelmed Latin America with an avalanche of products, introduced ready cash into a trade network long characterized and dominated by credit, so that local merchants were swamped by British traders with larger cash resources. "With dizzying speed the British destroyed an entire commercial system" (pp. 46-51). New York instead underwent a process of economic *de*colonization; and, as we have seen, enjoyed a thirty year period of remarkable economic growth, marred only briefly by such incidents as the Jeffersonian embargo of 1807 and the depression of 1819.

There is a genuine danger, of course, in concentrating excessively upon differences at the expense of similarities. Halperín-Donghi's belief that "altering the social structure was not among the direct objectives of any politically significant party" (p. 22) is equally true of the United States in the post-revolutionary period. Moreover a recent book by Joseph J. Ellis called *After the Revolution: Profiles of Early American Culture* (New York, 1979) corresponds in several key respects with Halperín-Donghi's thesis that "the somewhat blind optimism of 1810" gave way to fear, disappointment, and disquiet (p. vii). Nevertheless, on balance I am impressed by the genuine rapidity of change in early national New York, as demonstrable in spheres so diverse as new towns, architecture and law as in economic and demographic trends.[42] New York did not fulfill *all* of the Founding Fathers' expectations. No state possibly could. But the ebullient optimism expressed in 1825 at the completion of the Erie Canal should not be minimized as mere rhetoric or hyperbole.

---

42. See Mark DeWolfe Howe, "The Process of Outlawry in New York: A Study of the Selective Reception of English Law," in David H. Flaherty, ed., *Essays in the History of Early American Law* (Chapel Hill, 1969), 433-50; Steven R. Boyd, "The Impact of the Constitution on State Politics: New York as a Test Case," in James Kirby Martin, ed., *The Human Dimensions of Nation Making: Essays on Colonial and Revolutionary America* (Madison, Wisc., 1976), 270-303.

Did we live amidst ruins, which mark former greatness;—were we always presented with scenes indicating present decay...we might be as little inclined as others, to look forward. But we delight in the promised sunshine of the future, and leave to those who are conscious that they have passed their grand climacteric, to console themselves with the splendors of the past.[43]

The sentiments of Cadwallader D. Colden (Figure 5) on that august occasion were not merely the articulation of an American voice. Colden's most certainly was a *North* American voice; and, read in the full context of the *Celebration of the Completion of the New York Canals,* it was specifically a New York voice. By 1825, no other state had come so far, so fast in the previous four decades.

V

I cannot resist the temptation to add a postscript pertaining to a modern classic written by Dixon Ryan Fox while he served as president of this college. *Yankees and Yorkers* is one of the most delightful books ever written about New York history, and one of the most influential. In his last two chapters, where Fox treats the period that we have been surveying, he acknowledges the Yankee migration to and through New York, and of course the impact of Yankee culture upon New York. Nevertheless, Fox presumed and maintained the discreet viability of his stereotypical categories even two centuries, and more, after the initial founding of New Netherland and New England.

Viewed from one perspective, Fox's two types did persist.

---

43. Cadwallader D. Colden, *Memoir Prepared at the Request of a Committee of the Common Council of the City of New York . . . at the Celebration of the Completion of the New York Canals* (New York, 1825), 77-78.

5. Cadwallader David Colden *(1769-1834) by John Wesley Jarvis, ca. 1819, courtesy of the New York Historical Society.*

When Timothy Dwight visited here he found that "the people of Schenectady are descendants of the Dutch planters mixed with emigrants from Scotland, Ireland, England, and New England." Among the leading citizens of Schenectady, mostly clergymen, he found both Yankee and Yorker types. And why not? Between 1790 and 1820 the three states of southern New England lost approximately 800,000 people to westward migration. Most of them settled in or passed through New York. Nantucket whalers founded Hudson, New York, in 1783; and New Englanders laid out Troy in 1787. After 1807 the area west of Lake Champlain came to be called "New Vermont," and a majority of the participants in New York's Constitutional Convention of 1821 were men of New England stock.[44]

Still and all, those Yankees and Yorkers did two things that haven't been mentioned much but which mess up the tidiness of President Fox's rubrics. Some of them—especially the influential promoters and publicists—hopped back and forth from New York to New England. I'm thinking of Elkanah Watson (1758-1842), for example: merchant, canal promoter, and agriculturalist. Born of Pilgrim stock at Plymouth, Massachusetts, he toured Holland in 1784 and wrote an extremely perceptive book about his experiences, settled at Albany in 1789, organized a bank there and became a leading citizen. He promoted two canal companies and a stage coach line from Albany to Schenectady, fought for various local improvements, obtained a charter for the New York State Bank, and made out so well that he retired early and moved to Pittsfield, Massachusetts, in the Berkshires. Looking at the trajectory of Watson's career as well as his adaptive temperament, I cannot presume to call him Yankee or Yorker.

---

44. Dwight, *op. cit.*, II, 340-44; David M. Ellis, "The Yankee Invasion of New York, 1783-1850," *New York History*, 32 (Jan. 1951), 7-8, 13; Ellis, "Yankee-Dutch Confrontation in the Albany Area," *New England Quarterly*, 45 (June 1972), 262-70.

Next take the case of Jesse Buel (1778-1839). In 1796 he got released from his apprenticeship in Rutland, Vermont, and took himself to New York City where he found work as a journeyman printer. Beginning in 1797 he made a series of rapid vocational and geographical moves: to Albany, then Troy, then Poughkeepsie, then Kingston, and back to Albany in 1813 where he published his fifth weekly newspaper, *The Argus*. Would you call this son of Connecticut and Vermont a Yankee or a Yorker? What about Jedediah Barber (1787-1876), born in Connecticut, who came to New York State in 1804, settled in Homer in 1811 and opened his successful store, "The Great Western," in 1813? What about James and William Wadsworth of Connecticut, who became patriarchs of the Genesee country?[45] Or Judge Hugh White from Middletown, Connecticut, who colonized Whitestown, New York, in 1784? Or Samuel Kirkland of Connecticut who established the Hamilton-Oneida Academy? Or Charles Finney, yet another native of Connecticut raised in Utica?

The other thing that these migratory Yankees did was to breed with Yorkers. Rufus King of Massachusetts married Mary Alsop, daughter of a very wealthy dry goods merchant who had moved during the war from New York City to Middletown, Connecticut, and then back again. So many of these Yankee-Yorker marriages occurred—including Elbridge Gerry, Samuel Osgood, and even John Adams's daughter Abigail—that in 1786 Adams wrote to Rufus King a semi-facetious comment: "It will be unnatural if federal Purposes are not answered by all these Intermarriages."[46]

---

45. Carman, *op. cit.*, xv-xvii, xix, xxii; Herbert B. Howe, "Jedediah Barber, Merchant of Homer," *New York History*, 17 (July 1936), 290-305; Wright, *op. cit.*, 98.

46. Robert Ernst, *Rufus King: American Federalist* (Chapel Hill, 1968), 65-68. See also Wilbur Zelinsky, *The Cultural Geography of the United States* (Englewood Cliffs, N. J., 1973), 84, 121, 127; Helen M. Morgan, ed., *A Season in New York, 1801: Letters of Harriet and Maria Trumbull* (Pittsburgh, 1969); Clarence Cook, ed., *A Girl's Life Eighty Years Ago: Selections from the Letters of Eliza Southgate Bowne* (New York, 1888), 127-38, 150-235. Fox acknowledges the occurrence of intermarriage very briefly on p. 212.

Let's look at just one last family and be done. Jonathan Edwards, second son of the great theologian, grew up in Northampton and Stockbridge, Massachusetts; graduated from Princeton in 1765; studied theology with Joseph Bellamy at Bethlehem, Connecticut; and eventually became a less-than-successful pastor, first in New Haven and later at Colebrook, Connecticut. In 1799 he happily accepted the presidency of Union College, a post he held until his death in 1801.

William Edwards, born in Elizabethtown, New Jersey, in 1770, was a grandson of the same illustrious Jonathan Edwards (hence a nephew of the Jonathan just discussed). In 1789 he completed an apprenticeship in the tanning trade, returned to Northampton, built several tanneries, and developed various sorts of labor-saving devices as well as measures to improve the quality of leather. His business grew so rapidly that eventually he had five tanneries in operation around Northampton. Shady financial manipulations by his backers brought about bankruptcy in 1815. Two years later, however, assisted by his sons and some New York friends, he made a new start at Hunter, in Greene County, New York, where he built what became the largest tannery in the United States. His technical improvements reduced the cost of sole leather from twelve to four cents a pound; and he is recognized as the founder of the hide and leather industry in the United States.[47]

How are we to regard these people who in many instances enjoyed greater success in New York than in New England? What can we call the Yankees who prospered, married, and then raised children who remained in New York? (Let me bring to your attention the fact that the New England Society of New York was established as early as 1805.) Well, with all due respect to Dixon Ryan Fox and neat historical categories, we may need to contemplate such tongue-twisting designa-

---

47. William W. and William Henry Edwards, *Memoirs of Col. William Edwards* (Washington, D. C., 1897), 45-52, 67-82, 95-102.

tions as Yankers and Yorkees.[48] By 1825, when James Fenimore Cooper had just started writing his historical novels, the old stereotypes still persisted; but the characterological attributes, the local allegiances, and even the genetic pools had begun to be blended. Yankers and Yorkees? Yorkees and Yankers?

Think about it.

The author wishes to thank Glenn C. Altschuler, Richard L. Bushman, Paul W. Gates, Peter D. McClelland, and Mary Beth Norton for their helpful assessments of this essay and suggestions for its improvement.

48. If I seem excessively whimsical about tried and true labels, please recall that central New York was then known as "the land of silly names," that until 1809 Syracuse was called Bogardus Corners, and Auburn was known as Hardenburg Corners. I am only being faithful to the spirit of the times!

NOTES ON CONTRIBUTORS

MANFRED JONAS is Washington Irving Professor in Modern Literary and Historical Studies at Union College. Although primarily a diplomatic historian [*Isolationism in America 1935-1941* (1966), *American Foreign Relations in the Twentieth Century* (1967), *Roosevelt and Churchill: Their Secret Wartime Correspondence* (with F.L. Loewenheim and H.D. Langley, 1975)], his ventures into American colonial history include *Die Unabhängigkeitserklärung der Vereinigten Staaten* (1964), as well as articles in the *Maryland Historical Magazine* (1956), the *Essex Institute Historical Collections* (1960), and the *Jahrbuch fur Amerikastudien* (1966).

MICHAEL KAMMEN is Newton C. Farr Professor of American History and Culture at Cornell University. His *People of Paradox* (1972) won the Pulitzer Prize for History in 1973, and his numerous other publications include *Society, Freedom, and Conscience: The Coming of the Revolution in Virginia, Massachusetts and New York* (with J.P. Greene and R.L. Bushman, 1976) and *Colonial New York: A History* (1975). He served on the American Revolution Bicentennial Advisory Board of the American Association for State and Local History and the Board of Editors of *New York History,* and is currently on the Board of Trustees of the New York State Historical Association.

MARY-JO KLINE has served as associate editor for The Adams Papers, as assistant and associate editor for The John Jay Papers, and as editor for the Papers of Aaron Burr. Her varied publications include *Alexander Hamilton: A Biography in his own Words* (1973), *The Book of Abigail and John* (with L.H. Butterfield and M.Friedlaender, 1975), *The Papers of John Adams,* vols. 1 and 2 (with R.J. Taylor and G. Lint, 1977), and *Gouverneur Morris and the New Nation* (1978). She is currently preparing a guide to documentary editing under a grant from the National Endowment for the Humanities.

DONALD W. MEINIG is Maxwell Professor of Geography at Syracuse University. Though primarily known as a cultural geographer of the American West [*The Great Columbia Plain* (1968), *Imperial Texas* (1969), *Southwest, Three Peoples in Geographical Change* (1971)], he has increasingly turned his attention to the Northeast. He contributed three chapters on the historical development of New York to *Geography of New York State* (J. Thompson, ed., 1965) and expressed his deep interest in the interface between history and geography in "The Continuous Shaping of America: A Prospectus for Geographers and Historians," which appeared on the *American Historical Review* in 1978.

WILLIAM H. SILES is chief historian at Genesee Country Village, Mumford, N. Y. He has been Coordinator of the Study Center for Early Religious Life in Western New York State at Ithaca College and has taught both at the University of Massachusetts, Amherst, and the State University of New York at Albany. His numerous conference papers include "Genesee Country Settlement: Economic Opportunity and the Safety Valve Thesis" (1978), "Oliver Phelps, Entrepreneur, and the Peopling of New York" (1979), and "Revivalism in Central New York: Whitney Cross and Burned-Over Distict History" (1980).

ROBERT V. WELLS is professor of History at Union College. The author of *The Population of the British Colonies in America before 1776* (1975) and *Revolutions in American's Lives: A Demographic Perspective on the History of Americans, Their Families, and Their Society* (1982), his writings in family and demographic history, particularly of the colonial period, have appeared in numerous composite volumes as well as the *New York Historical Society Quarterly* (1973), the *Journal of Social History* (1975), and the *Journal of Interdisciplinary History* (1974 and 1978). He served as consultant on population for the *Atlas of Early American History* (1976).